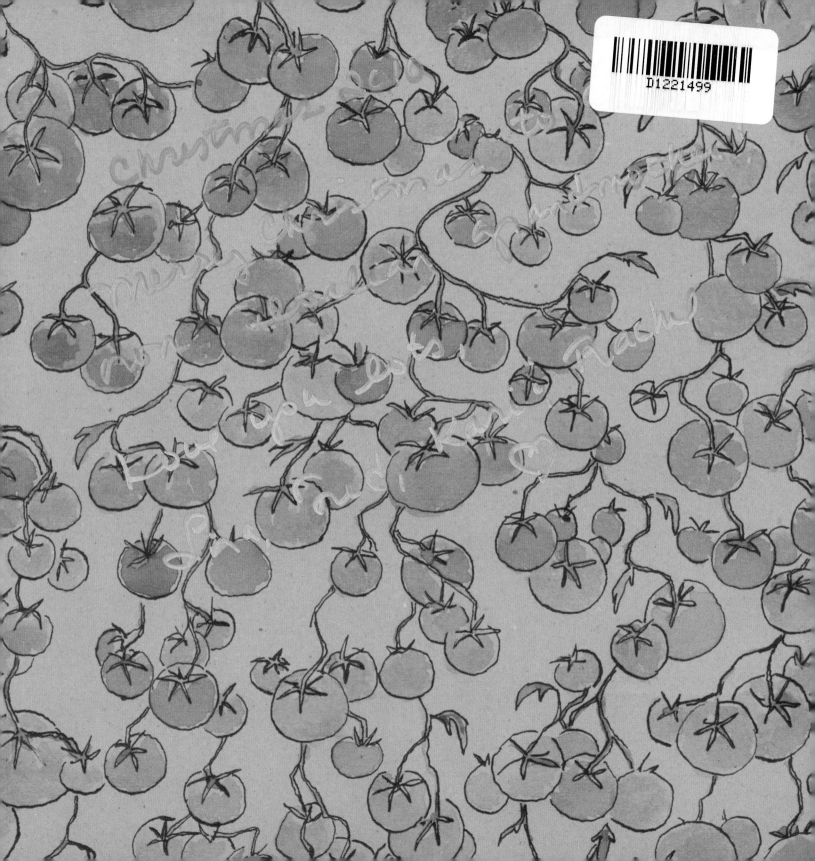

"No one who cooks, cooks alone. Even at her
most solitary, a cook in the kitchen is surrounded by
generations of cooks past, the advice and menus
of cooks present, the wisdom of cookbook writers."

Laurie Colwin, *writer*

Cooking with Italian Grandmothers

Recipes and Stories from Tuscany to Sicily

JESSICA THEROUX
INTRODUCTION BY ALICE WATERS

ILLUSTRATIONS BY ZACH HEWITT · EDITED BY KATRINA FRIED

welcome
BOOKS

NEW YORK

CONTENTS

FOREWORD

Jessica Theroux

This is a book about women and food and listening.

The art of good cooking lies in paying close care and attention. I learned this in Italy, from the mothers and grandmothers whose homes and kitchens I lived in for more than a year. I learned this from Carluccia and her beans, from Usha and her buttery cakes, from Armida and her chickens, from the cycles of the seasons, from the daily and seasonal hunger and plenty that comes with living close to the land. Good cooking, the kind that feeds the soul and nourishes the body, is the result of listening openly and acting simply. All of the women in this book taught me something about the power of food to connect us; to ourselves, our history, our land, our culture, to our past and to the present moment.

Prior to going to Italy, my cooking had focused on food's ability to heal, both physically and psychologically. Curing an intense childhood illness through diet and herbs at the age of eleven had proven to me the centrality of food for wellbeing. This pivotal experience compelled me to focus on cooking delicious, nutrient-dense food as a livelihood. I went to Italy after spending a number of years working with healing foods because I knew that there were other important things I needed to learn; in particular, I wanted to explore how food embodies our personal and collective histories. Who better to teach me this than the grandmothers of Italy, a country that deeply values and protects its food traditions; a country that's culture revolves largely around the kitchen table.

People often ask me how I found the twelve women who I documented during my travels. My method was simple: I flew to Italy with a few personal contacts, and those provided through the organization Slow Food, and trusted that I would find what I needed once I was there. The year began with these referrals, which then developed into more referrals. As time passed, and I became more confident, I also started to move to the towns or regions I was drawn to. I would find a room to rent and then begin asking around for the area's beloved female elders. Directions were followed along dirt roads and to front doors, where I introduced myself and my work, and was then warmly welcomed in for the next big meal.

I learned many of the recipes in this book from the grandmothers I met. Others were created in response to a given woman's cooking style, favorite ingredients, or the mood and sensibility that her character evoked for me. In keeping with my background and training, the recipes and menus have been developed with an eye towards balance and nourishment.

My greatest hope is that this book will encourage you to pay the utmost attention to your life, and in particular to your food and the people around you. What you discover could change your life.

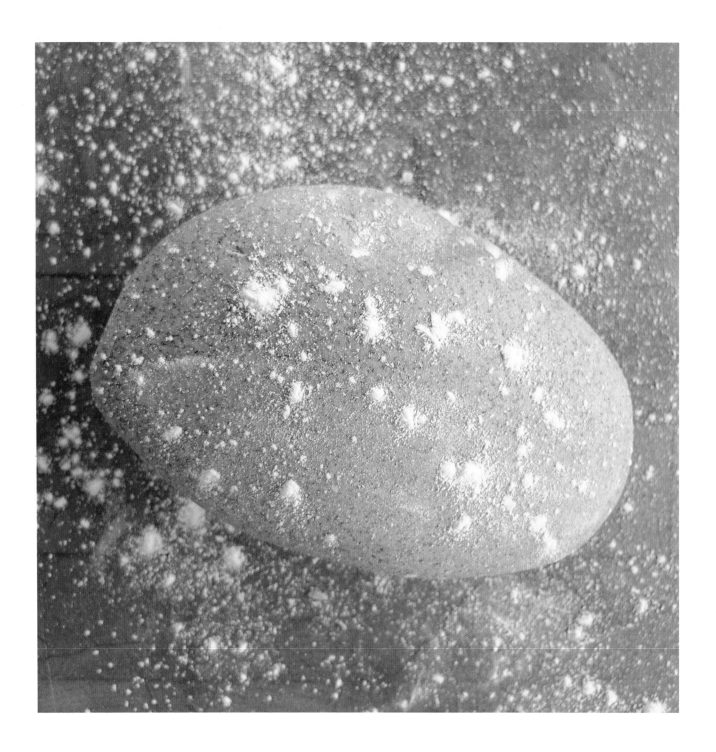

INTRODUCTION

Alice Waters

Cooking with Italian Grandmothers begins the important work of documenting the simple traditions that have been passed down verbally through generations. Grandmothers are the guardians of our collective culture and their secrets and techniques are as relevant now as they were a hundred years ago. We have forgotten how to feed ourselves and each other and are at risk of losing our culinary heritage. However, when the stories are told and the recipes retained, we somehow manage to secure them for the future.

There is a wealth of knowledge and wisdom in the simple food traditions of the elder generation all around the world. Every society shares these same roots and in Italy it is particularly strong. Women rich or poor are still connected to the land; they cook seasonally, humbly, and with care. Jessica Theroux has taken a gift for connecting with people and new cultures and translated it into an anthology of stories that capture the role of food and family in the lives of twelve remarkable women. Her closeness with the women she has lived and cooked with comes through with clarity and beauty as we meet them through their pasta, beans, and rabbits.

Even considering Italians' enthusiastic embrace of those interested in their food, not every cook could arrive at a doorstep in a foreign land, weary and travel worn, and so seamlessly integrate themselves into a stranger's life, and a family's rhythm. With each woman that Jessica encounters, we see the love, care and a mutual admiration that opens the door to an exchange of knowledge with the keepers of an invaluable cultural legacy.

We are beginning to wake up to a new appreciation of the value of food traditions, and not a moment too soon. For decades we have systematically delivered the message that food is fuel, and that cooking is drudgery. This mindset has put into peril the wealth of wisdom built over generations: delicious ways to preserve the summer bounty for the winter months, how to cook beans grown in one field differently than the drier beans grown in another, hundreds of ways to nourish ourselves in the most basic way.

Years ago Jessica put several of the wonderfully simple recipes now in this book to work in my own kitchen with beautiful results. She is a talented cook, writer, and documentarian. *Cooking with Italian Grandmothers* is an exquisite, heartfelt anthology that is an important reference for us all.

Dedicated to Grandma Honey,

for loving and believing in me whole-heartedly and without reserve.

May we all love and be loved in such a way at some point in our lives.

J.T.

Mamma Maria

Devi fare le cose con calma, una per volta.

Things must be done calmly, bit by bit.

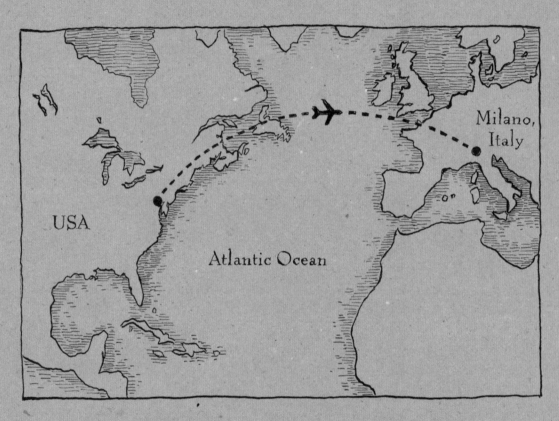

Milano, Lombardia

It began in 1987 with a shoe full of strawberries.

I was eight. My mother, sister, and I had traveled to Milan for the wedding of our *au pair*, Graziella, to Beppe. There was dancing and sweet chaos, multicolored rice thrown at Graziella as she walked out of the church.

Late in the evening my dessert of wine-soaked strawberries fell into my blue shoe, and I decided to eat them anyway, plucking them out one at a time. Those strawberries were boozy and sweet, exotic and delicious. They got me hooked: These Italians seemed to know something about having fun.

There's a rumor that after the wedding Graziella chopped off the bottom of her wedding dress and dyed it red, so that she could go out dancing in it. I thought she was so racy! As our *au pair*, she would make us crispy white toast slathered with Italian chocolate on dreary London mornings. Chocolate and hazelnuts from the north of Italy, creamed together with sugar and fat. It was pure decadence for an English schoolgirl.

On another trip to Milan when I was four, my sister and I stayed with Graziella's mother, Mamma Maria, while our parents toured the rest of Italy. I remember vividly the hours we spent propped up in our chairs at her kitchen table, sticky from the summer heat, waiting eagerly for Mamma Maria to bring out the next warm, soft dish. Her kitchen seemed endlessly filled with smells and flavors to comfort and distract us from missing our parents: soups swimming with tiny pastas, creamy curdled eggs, and countless numbers of cookies made moist from being dipped in milk.

It seems to me now that I was always destined to return to Italy someday to recapture those childhood pleasures.

"Mamma Maria was the original Italian grandmother for me, and it made complete sense to go back to that beginning."

Left: Me, age four, with Mamma Maria.
Opposite: One of Milan's many *palazzi*.

Mamma Maria was the original Italian grandmother for me, and as I set out as a young chef to document and learn Italy's food traditions, it made complete sense to go back to that beginning and stay with her first.

My mother had dug up an old phone number for Mamma Maria, and early one morning I sat down to call her. I was greeted at the other end of the phone by her familiar *"Pronto!"* Instead of answering the telephone with *ciao*—the English equivalent of "hello"—Italians typically say *pronto*, "I'm ready." It struck me that morning how especially fitting that expression was for Mamma Maria. She was always ready. The beds were ready for sleep each night, with their ironed sheets folded tightly under the mattress and their pillows perfectly fluffed. The dusky pink bathroom was pristinely clean, with even the toilet paper folded perfectly on the roll for the next person (how did she keep up with this?). Food was cooked ahead of time, and the pots and pans were put away before anyone arrived for the meal. Yes, Mamma Maria had life in order. She was prepared.

So it was settled. I would start my journey with Mamma Maria, and then hatch a plan for where to go next after I'd adjusted to the Italian way of life with her. I hoped to spend the next year following my taste buds through the kitchens of Italy's beloved grandmothers. I was convinced that I needed to learn about food in a country whose culture centered on cooking and eating. I also yearned for the sense of nurture and connection that comes with being well fed; I wanted to experience this, and I wanted to learn how to do this for others.

I arrived in Milan at 8:30 a.m. on a Sunday. Graziella was there to meet me as promised, identifiable by her glasses and long brown hair. She had basically not aged in the fifteen years that

had passed since I last saw her. The ride home was sweet, filled with questions about each of our families, and at moments some confusion over what exactly was being said.

When we arrived at Mamma Maria's she welcomed me with an excited smile and a warm hug. I was struck by how familiar everything was: The smells, the sounds, the way everything looked was just as I'd remembered.

My first night there we talked at length about Lombardian cooking, the foods Mamma Maria ate as a girl, and the ways in which things had changed since her childhood. Rather than the abundance of the current Italian meal structure, with its multiple courses and dishes, Mamma Maria was raised on meals that comprised either a starch and vegetable, or a protein and vegetable.

It occurred to me that one of the effects of the enforced wartime simplicity was an essentially rather healthful lifestyle. Modest meals were eaten at night, and stronger foods were consumed earlier in the day, when more energy was needed for active work. There was an intimate dependence on one's garden, on the local trees, on the land and the ocean, on the animals one raised, and on the foods and skills one could trade with neighbors. This type of interconnectedness was also mimicked in the family structure. "In the past, when you married, you would go live with your mother-in-law and your husband's family," explained Mamma Maria. "No one moved into a place alone."

Mamma Maria's mother was known by all as an incredible cook, and one who could make a delicious meal out of whatever was at hand, however plentiful or meager. On Sundays, she would kill a chicken for the family meal—Sunday was "chicken killing and eating day," according to Mamma Maria. In addition to chicken day, there was also "a day for eating eggs each week—eggs in frittata, eggs cooked in warm tomatoes, eggs cooked many ways." Each autumn Mamma Maria and her mother would help to slaughter and butcher the family's pigs for fresh and cured meat. The special meals were those that contained animal protein; one of Mamma Maria's favorite child-hood meals was stuffed pigs' feet with home-grown potato puree.

Mamma Maria learned to cook at her mother's side. "You just watch and spend time. You lend a hand. Maybe the first time you make a mistake, then the second time you do it right. It's not that you are 'taught.'" This was, of course, what I'd come to Italy to do—to spend time with

Clockwise from top left: The *Duomo di Milano,* Milan's cathedral. Mamma Maria in her kitchen. The view out Mamma Maria's kitchen window. A view of the vegetable market from Mamma Maria's balcony.

"This was what I'd come to Italy to do—spend time with women like Mamma Maria, listen to their stories, drink a lot of *espresso*, and make meal after meal at the their sides."

Mamma Maria's mother with other local cooks.

women like Mamma Maria, listen to their stories, drink a lot of *espresso*, watch them cook, and make meal after meal at their sides.

My first morning with Mamma Maria was typical of those to come. The double doors to the balcony off the kitchen were open, and city sounds and birdsong drifted into the room. Mamma Maria was in there, waiting for me to arrive in my bathrobe and the purple slippers she had bought especially for my visit. The *espresso* pot began to bubble and hiss as I walked through the door, and the full-fat milk followed shortly behind. A selection of *biscotti* was laid carefully on a plate. It was breakfast time.

After talking briefly about the night's sleep, we got right to planning what we would cook together over the coming weeks. We mapped the whole thing out: *involtini* and *polenta* (her mother's best dishes), *Cotolette alla Milanese*, and perhaps *Risotta alla Milanese* (we were, after all, in Milan). Mamma Maria did not like to dirty her kitchen too much, and these were rather involved recipes, so we would take our time and pace ourselves with all the cooking. Besides, one of the most important things I learned from Mamma Maria is that you have to do things with calm. Whenever we were in the kitchen she would say, "*Devi fare le cose con calma. Una per volta.*"

As Mamma Maria and I cooked these Lombardian dishes together I started to get a better sense of Northern Italian cuisine. These dishes were heavy, warming, and very sturdy. Mamma Maria was like this, too—substantial and soft in stature, with a big heart and a routine that was easy to rest into. The whole thing was turning out to be very soothing.

So what was it about the *involtini*, the *polenta*, the *risotto*s and braises that warmed my belly for so many hours and grounded me in such a strong way? I think the slow, long cooking contracted the flavors of each dish, and allowed the food to absorb the deep gentle heat. The *involtini* simmered gently in tomato sauce for a good hour, the *polenta* cooked for at least forty minutes, and the braised veal shanks tenderized slowly over hours in a barely bubbling mixture of wine, broth, vegetables, and herbs.

Beyond the cooking methods, which are really best suited to wintertime, Lombardian cuisine also employs a lot of red meat and dairy. These animal products tend to be more concentrated in energy and therefore heartier. After years of being a vegetarian prior to living in Italy, these foods made me feel as though I were sinking into a large, comfortable sofa. It was noticeable, and in the best way possible.

After two weeks of cooking with Mamma Maria, I had mastered the basics of Lombardian cusine and added two inches to my waistline. My year in Italy was already proving to be growthful on many fronts, and it was time to start thinking about where I would go next. As Mamma Maria and I talked over the different possibilities, her concern for my life as a single woman in Italy began to grow. I should not travel to the south without a man. No way. Her furrowed brow communicated what her words did not. The Lombardians are sincere, southerners are not. We decided it would be best for me to go instead to the Lake Como region. It was only a short drive from Milan, and was supposed to be a pretty place with good local food. They cooked with some of my favorite ingredients—buckwheat, cabbage, and winter squash—all accompanied by browned butter and sage.

In preparation for my travels, Mamma Maria gave me a special present: starched white pajamas covered in lace and yellow polka dots. They were packaged neatly in a plastic bag. She must have bought them for me in the market below her house. They were "in case I needed to look good for bed." Interesting. We tucked these oddly childish pajamas into the suitcase Mamma Maria had packed with all of my perfectly ironed clothes. The purple slippers were almost ready to come off. All that was missing was a last bit of advice, given over a shot of *espresso*:

"Prendi una bella viletta con giardino. E bambini. È la prima cosa che quando ti sposi—prendi i soldini avete e trovi una bella casettina con orto. Allora, ti vengo a trovare!"

(Get a beautiful little house with a garden. And children. It's the first thing you should do when you marry—gather together all the money you have and find a beautiful little home with a vegetable garden. So, go find it!)

MAMMA MARIA : MILANO, LOMBARDIA

MENU ONE

Involtini di Milano
(Slow-Braised Meat Rolls from the Province of Milan)

Polenta with Warm Cream and Gorgonzola

Roasted Apples with Hazelnut, Bitter Chocolate, and Lemon Zest

MENU TWO

Osso Buco
(Wine-and-Herb-Braised Veal Shanks with *Gremolata*)

Risotto alla Milanese
(Saffron *Risotto*)

MENU THREE

Cotolette alla Milanese
(Pan-Seared Breaded Veal Cutlets with *Salsa Verde*)

Crushed Baby Potatoes with Lemon and Chives

Spinaci con Aglio, Olio, e Peperoncino
(Spinach with Garlic, Olive Oil, and Hot Pepper)

Fragole al Vino
(Wine-Soaked Strawberries with Whipped Cream)

Menu One

Involtini di Milano (Slow-Braised Meat Rolls from the Province of Milan)
Serves 6–8

Both Mamma Maria and her mother were known for their *involtini*. Mamma Maria prefers to roll her ground meat filling in thin slices of beef, the way she learned during her childhood in the Lombardian province of Pavia. However, around Milan it is also common to roll the filling into blanched and de-stemmed savoy cabbage leaves before slowly simmering them in tomato sauce. If you try the *involtini* rolled in cabbage, make sure to secure them well with kitchen twine rather than the toothpicks. *Involtini* is one of Mamma Maria's favorite dishes to make, in part because you can cook the *involtini* the day before and then reheat them, making for a cleaner kitchen and less fuss at mealtime. Mamma Maria makes her *involtini* with *polenta* on winter Sundays, when her daughters and their children are over for lunch.

For the *involtini* rolls:
4 ounces ground pork
2 ounces ground chicken
8 ounces ground beef
¼ cup finely grated Parmesan
6 tablespoons plain bread crumbs
2 large eggs
¼ cup minced parsley
½ teaspoon salt
½ teaspoon black pepper
*1½ pounds raw slices beef top sirloin,
    roughly 12–15 slices, pounded to ⅛"
    thickness and at least 2½ x 3" in size*

For the sauce:
3 tablespoons olive oil
3 whole cloves garlic, peeled
1 onion, finely diced
1 carrot, finely diced
2 bay leaves
¼ cup red or white wine
2 cups tomato puree
2 cups beef broth
½ teaspoon salt

To make the filling for the meat rolls, knead together the ground pork, chicken, beef, Parmesan, bread crumbs, eggs, parsley, salt, and black pepper.

Lay a slice of the beef top sirloin on a cutting board, and place a couple of spoonfuls of the filling at one end. Roll the filling up into the beef, making sure to tuck in the sides as you go.

Secure the roll with a toothpick skewered all the way through the middle of the roll. Repeat this procedure for the rest of the slices and filling.

For the sauce, heat the olive oil over medium-high heat in a wide pot until it starts to shimmer. Brown the *involtini* in batches, on all sides, and set them aside on a plate when nicely caramelized. Turn down the heat to medium, and sauté the garlic cloves, onion, carrot, and bay leaves in the remaining oil. Add the wine, scraping loose any brown sticky bits from the bottom of the pan, and then the tomato puree, broth, and salt.

Return the *involtini* and their juices to the pot, bring to a simmer, and cover with a lid set slightly ajar. Simmer the meat rolls gently for about 1½ hours, turning the *involtini* a few times during cooking.

Serve over Mamma Maria's *Polenta* with Warm Cream and Gorgonzola.

Polenta with Warm Cream and Gorgonzola

Serves 6–8

Polenta is typically a winter dish. Not only does it warm the belly, but constantly stirring a pot of simmering cornmeal takes strength and stamina, generating a lot of heat for the cook. There are many ways Mamma Maria recommends eating *polenta*: with *involtini*; with a simple red sauce, cheese, or salt cod if finances are tight; or, as in her childhood, with little stewed wild birds.

Mamma Maria's *polenta* has a lot of give; if it is looking too thick, you can always add a bit of warm milk or water, and if it's too thin, more dry *polenta* can be stirred in. It's flexible that way and easy on the cook. When it starts to thicken, switch to a wooden spoon for the stirring. Mamma Maria serves her *polenta* soft, right off the stove, with warm cream sauce, a hunk of local Gorgonzola cheese, and topped with *involtini*. Generally, it takes about forty minutes for the *polenta* to lose its graininess and become fully fragrant, although I like Mamma Maria's belief that "it's done when the people arrive."

For the *polenta*:
10 cups water
1 teaspoon salt
Spoonful of olive oil
2 cups coarsely ground yellow polenta

For the warm cream and Gorgonzola:
2 tablespoons (¼ stick) salted butter
¾ cup heavy cream
¼ pound Gorgonzola cheese

Bring the water to a rolling boil in a large, heavy pot. Add the salt and spoonful of olive oil. Let the *polenta* slowly "rain" into the boiling water, whisking constantly. Reduce the heat to a simmer. Switch to a long-handled wooden spoon, and stir constantly along the bottom and sides of the pot. The *polenta* is done when it pulls away from the side of the pot in one mass (about 40 minutes). At this point it will have lost its graininess and become very fragrant.

For a less labor-intensive version of Mamma Maria's *polenta*, you can cover the pot with a lid during the cooking; every 10 minutes, stir the polenta for a full 2 minutes. It will be done in roughly 50 minutes.

Warm the butter and cream together in a saucepan set over low heat, whisking to combine. Simmer for 5 minutes to slightly reduce and thicken.

To serve, ladle the *polenta* onto plates, spoon the warm cream sauce over it, place a slice of Gorgonzola on top, and finish with the *involtini* and sauce.

Roasted Apples with Hazelnut, Bitter Chocolate, and Lemon Zest

Serves 6

Proud and compact, Mamma Maria and her *involtini* provided the inspiration for these plump filled apples. I developed this recipe to suit many varieties of apples, though my preference is to use a tart fruit such as the Granny Smith. These are the most delicious roasted apples I have eaten, with the bitter chocolate (typical of Northern Italy) and lemon zest adding depth and brightness. I recommend using a chocolate with eighty percent cocoa content for this recipe.

6 firm baking apples (such as Granny Smith, Pink Lady, Crispin, or Pippin)
¼ cup sugar, divided
¼ cup (½ stick) soft unsalted butter, plus more for greasing
2 teaspoons finely grated or minced lemon zest
⅔ cup finely chopped toasted hazelnuts
2 ounces (⅓ cup) chopped dark chocolate (I use 80 percent cocoa content)
1½ cups sweet Marsala wine, divided

Optional accompaniment:
Softly whipped heavy cream, unsweetened

Preheat the oven to 375 degrees F. Butter a small baking dish, roughly 8 by 10 inches.

Slice a thin layer off the bottom of the apples and discard; this levels the apples out so that they have a stable base upon which to stand during roasting. Slice ½ inch off the tops of the apples, and set the tops to one side. Peel the apple bases. Then, using a small teaspoon, scrape out an inch-diameter core from each apple, making sure not to cut through the bottom.

Mix together 3 tablespoons of the sugar with the butter, lemon zest, hazelnuts, and chocolate. Spoon this filling into the center of the apples, mounding any extra on top. Drizzle the exposed apples with the ¾ cup of the Marsala, and cover them with their tops. Pour the rest of the Marsala over the apples and sprinkle them with the remaining 1 tablespoon sugar.

Bake for 45 minutes, basting the apples with the hot Marsala a few times during their roasting. The apples are done when a toothpick can be inserted into them easily. Serve warm, with Marsala spooned over the apples and whipped cream on the side.

Osso Buco (Wine-and-Herb-Braised Veal Shanks with *Gremolata*)
Serves 6

Slowly simmering shanks of veal in wine and broth creates a winter dish that's grounding and warming—the trademarks of Mamma Maria's cooking. She first made me this dish when I was four, and I remember the shock of the big bone and its gooey, musky marrow. I adjusted her version of *osso buco* to be in *bianco* (tomato-less), bringing the dish closer to its historic roots with the addition of cinnamon, allspice, and a garnish of *gremolata* (minced citrus zest, parsley, and garlic). The further addition of fresh herbs imparts welcome earthy and floral undertones, pairing this dish well with its classic accompaniment of *Risotto alla Milanese*.

6 veal shanks, 8–10 ounces each
½ teaspoon salt
3 tablespoons vegetable oil or lard, divided
2½ cups dry white wine, divided
2 tablespoons (¼ stick) unsalted butter
2 medium yellow onions, diced small
3 carrots, peeled and diced small
2 stalks celery, peeled and diced small
7 medium garlic cloves, left whole, smashed with the back of a knife
1 strip lemon zest, no white
3 bay leaves
10 large sprigs fresh thyme, left whole, or ½ teaspoon dried
5 sprigs parsley, left whole
½ cinnamon stick
2 whole allspice berries, or a pinch of ground
3 cups chicken broth, preferably organic
Salt
Freshly ground white or black pepper

For the *gremolata*:
¼ cup finely minced parsley
2 small to medium cloves garlic, very finely minced
2 teaspoons very finely minced or grated organic orange zest

Preheat the oven to 325 degees F, and adjust the rack to the lower third of the oven.

Pat the shanks dry, and tie them tightly around their equators with cooking twine. Sprinkle them on both sides with salt (about ½ teaspoon total).

Heat 1½ tablespoons of the oil or lard in a large, heavy-bottomed pot (you want to use a pot with a lid) set over medium-high heat. When the oil begins to shimmer, sear three of the shanks until golden brown (about 5 minutes), then flip and sear the other side until browned (another 5 minutes). Remove from the pan and set aside in a large bowl. Add ¼ cup of the wine to the pan, stirring the bottom to loosen and dissolve any browned bits. Pour the wine over the veal shanks.

Return the pot to the burner, set over medium-high heat. Let it sit for a minute, so that any remaining liquid evaporates, then add the remaining 1½ tablespoons of oil or lard and sear the remaining three shanks according to the above procedure. When they have browned on both sides, remove them from the pan and deglaze it with another ¼ cup wine, pouring it over the shanks afterward.

Once again, return the pot to medium-high heat. Add the butter. When it has melted, add the onions, carrots, celery, garlic cloves, lemon zest, and all of the herbs and spices. Sauté until softened, about 10 minutes. Turn the heat up to high, and add the chicken broth and remaining 2 cups of wine. Add the veal shanks and juices, evenly distributing them in the pot.

Bring the liquid to a simmer and place the pot in the oven, with the lid slightly ajar. Bake for about 2 hours, turning the meat a few times during the cooking time. The shanks are done when they are tender and easily pierced with a fork. Remove the bay leaves, cinnamon stick, whole allspice berries, thyme branches, parsley stems, and garlic cloves. The sauce should have a loose-creamy consistency; if it's too brothy, reduce it by boiling, uncovered, over high heat. When the sauce has reached the desired consistency, taste for salt, adding more if necessary.

To make the *gremolata*, combine the parsley, garlic, and orange zest. Add half of the *gremolata* and a large pinch of pepper to the sauce.

Cut the kitchen twine off the shanks. Serve the *osso buco* with a small ladleful of sauce poured over the top, and a sprinkling of the remaining *gremolata* to finish. Remember to suck the marrow out of the bones; for many they are the most anticipated part of this dish.

Risotto alla Milanese (Saffron Risotto)
Serves 6

The secret to this simple *risotto* is adding the broth to the rice in small quantities, stirring constantly between the additions. It is the only way to achieve the ideal *risotto* texture: the rice grains tender and with a slight bite, clinging together through the creaminess that the slowly released starch provides. *Risotto* rice varieties differ in the amount of liquid they absorb, so feel free to add either less broth or more hot water if needed.

½ teaspoon loosely packed saffron threads
3 cups chicken broth, preferably organic
3 cups water
1½ cups dry white wine
6 tablespoons (¾ stick) unsalted butter, divided

1 large yellow onion, finely minced
Salt
2 cups risotto rice (Carnaroli or Arborio)
¾ cup finely grated Parmesan, divided
Coarsely ground black pepper

Toast the saffron threads in a skillet set over medium-low heat until they crumble easily between your fingers, about 3 to 4 minutes. Remove from the skillet and set aside.

Bring the broth, water, and wine to a simmer in a medium saucepan set over medium heat. When the liquid begins to simmer, lower the burner to the lowest possible setting and cover it with a lid—it should be just barely simmering.

Melt ¼ cup of the butter in a wide-bottomed saucepan or pot set over medium heat. Add the minced onion and a generous pinch of salt. Sauté until the onion has become very soft and translucent, 10 to 12 minutes. Crumble in the saffron and stir to distribute evenly. Add all of the rice and stir frequently until the edges of the rice start to become translucent, 3 to 5 minutes.

Add a ladleful (½ cup) of the warm broth to the rice, stirring constantly until the liquid has all been absorbed and the rice has become sticky. Repeat this procedure, one ladleful at a time, until the rice is tender, yet still with a bite, about 20 to 25 minutes, depending on how firm you like your risotto rice.

Turn off the heat and stir in the remaining 2 tablespoons butter and ½ cup Parmesan. Taste for salt, adding more if necessary. Serve garnished with the remaining ¼ cup Parmesan and a sprinkling of coarsely ground black pepper.

Cotolette alla Milanese (Pan-Seared Breaded Veal Cutlets with *Salsa Verde*)
Serves 6

For the *salsa verde*:
*1 cup tightly packed parsley with a few
   tablespoons fresh thyme or tarragon
   destemmed, washed, and dried
1 tablespoon finely minced shallot
   or red onion
2 teaspoons sherry or wine vinegar
1 tablespoon capers, rinsed
⅓ cup olive oil
Pinch of coarsely ground black pepper
⅛–½ teaspoon salt, depending on
   how salty your capers are*

For the *cotelette*:
*6 veal scallops or chops, about ¼" thick
½ teaspoon salt
3 large eggs, beaten
1½ cups bread crumbs
2 tablespoons olive oil or lard, plus more
   if necessary
Salt (preferably a flaky sea salt)
Freshly ground black pepper
1 lemon, cut into six wedges*

To prepare the *salsa verde*, combine the shallot and vinegar in a bowl and set aside for 15 minutes. Chop the herbs and capers together, leaving part of the mixture coarse while continuing to mince the rest to a texture of fine specks. Combine the herbs and capers with the shallot. Stir in enough olive oil to just cover the herbs, then mix to combine. Finally, stir in a pinch of black pepper and taste for salt, adding more if necessary.

Lightly season the cutlets on each side with the salt. Pass them first through the beaten eggs, and then the bread crumbs.

Heat the oil or lard in a skillet over medium-high heat. When the fat starts to shimmer, add the cutlets, cooking them in batches so as to not overcrowd the pan. Flip the cutlets when the first side has browned, 2 to 3 minutes, and brown the second side, adding more oil to the pan if necessary. Be careful not to overcook the cutlets—they should be a rosy pink in the center. The idea is to cook them quickly over high heat, so as to sear and crisp the outside. Remove them from the skillet, place on a warm platter, and sprinkle with a little sea salt and pepper.

Serve with lemon wedges and *salsa verde* on the side.

Crushed Baby Potatoes with Lemon and Chives
Serves 6–8

I prefer to use very small, waxy-skinned potatoes for this dish, such as the ubiquitous baby new potatoes or fingerlings. In addition to being a perfect compliment to the richness of the *cotolette*, these lemony potatoes go very well with many of the meat dishes in the book; in particular, I encourage you to try them as a side dish for Carluccia's Braised Goat Shoulder.

2½ pounds baby potatoes
2 tablespoons lemon juice
¼ cup olive oil
3 tablespoon minced chives
Salt

Place the potatoes in a pot of cold, salted water. Bring to a boil and simmer until pierced easily with a knife, 10 to 15 minutes. Strain, and place in a large mixing bowl. Gently crush the potatoes with the tines of a fork. Toss first with the lemon juice and then the olive oil and chives. Taste for salt, adding more if desired.

Spinaci con Aglio, Olio, e Peperoncino
(Spinach with Garlic, Olive Oil, and Hot Pepper)
Serves 6

Spinach sautéed with garlic, hot pepper, and olive oil is a classic Italian *contorno* (side dish), appearing throughout the north and south of the country. Almost every grandmother I met in Italy made a version of this sautéed spinach, and ultimately I chose Mamma Maria's because of how nicely its spicy softness complements the crispy *cotolette*. One important note about spinach: Be sure to serve it with a squeeze of lemon juice. The lemon adds a little acidity to the *cotolette* and neutralizes the naturally occurring oxalic acid in the spinach, increasing its calcium availability and boosting its taste.

2 pounds spinach
2 tablespoons olive oil
2 cloves garlic, cut in thin slivers
Small pinch of dried hot pepper flakes
Salt
1 lemon, cut into 6 wedges

Soak the spinach in a few batches of fresh water. To remove any sand or dirt, strain the spinach between batches by lifting it out of the water and into a colander. Once the spinach is clean, shake it briefly to remove excess liquid, though you want it to remain a little damp.

Warm the oil in a large, wide pot set over low heat. Add the garlic and hot pepper flakes, and sauté until the garlic begins turning golden brown. Add the slightly wet spinach and a couple of pinches of salt. Turn up the heat to high, and sauté until the spinach has turned emerald green and the water has evaporated.

Serve with the lemon wedges, to be squeezed onto the spinach just before eating.

Fragole al Vino (Wine-Soaked Strawberries with Whipped Cream)
Serves 6–8

In my ideal world, late springtime would be spent foraging for and eating bowlfuls of tiny forest strawberries. Lightly sprinkling strawberries with sugar and loosening them with a splash of good red wine creates the boozy exotic dish of my childhood. An alternative to the alcoholic version is to simply serve the berries with a chug of thick cream and a sprinkling of sugar on top.

4 cups ripe organic strawberries
2 tablespoons cane sugar
1 cup red wine
Whipping cream or vanilla ice cream to accompany

Gently clean the strawberries by briefly rinsing them, or wiping them with a soft cloth. Cut large strawberries lengthwise into halves or quarters; leave small ones whole. Sprinkle the berries with sugar, and pour the wine atop. Serve immediately, or leave the berries to soak in the fridge for a few hours to allow the flavors to develop. These strawberries are delicious with a dollop of unsweetened whipped cream, or a scoop of vanilla ice cream.

Giovanna

La cucina è per passione

The kitchen is for passion.

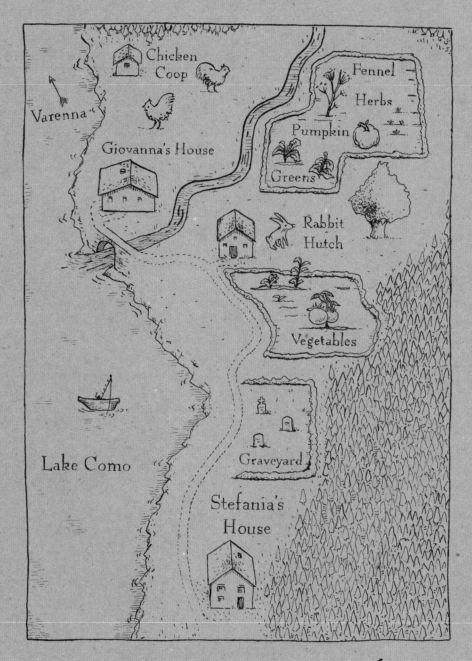

Chicken Coop

Varenna

Giovanna's House

Fennel

Herbs

Pumpkin

Greens

Rabbit Hutch

Vegetables

Lake Como

Graveyard

Stefania's House

Lago di Como, Lombardia

You never know who you'll meet. Or how that might change what happens next. On my flight to Italy I sat next to Heather, a friendly, middle-aged American woman making her annual visit to friends living on the shores of Lake Como. She went on and on about the Lombardian aunt Giovanna's cooking—earthy buckwheat noodles dressed with sweet pumpkin, bread pudding with pears and dried plums, baked in the glowing embers of the hearth, and a simple chocolate cake named after a nearby mountain, Grigna. She said that I must go and stay with her friend Stefania and cook with *Zia* Giovanna. Heather and I exchanged e-mail addresses, and the next day I received an introduction to Stefania, complete with the telephone number and street address for her family.

The day after my second serving of strawberries and wine with Mamma Maria in Milan, I picked up my leased car and drove away from the hustle and bustle of Italian city life. Lake Como appeared after two hours of driving past small towns and stores displaying the inflatable water toys necessary to partake of the lake's summer joys. Stefania was at her house to greet me when I arrived, and showed me to my bedroom. I was to stay for a week, and on first impression I felt safe with Stefania, her husband, and her son. This was of great relief; as a young woman traveling alone in Italy, it can be a bit dicey showing up at a stranger's house for the night.

Late in the afternoon, Stefania and I walked along a hillside path to her family's land. We passed her ancestors' graveyard, perched precariously on the edge of the hill, and as we neared the house we heard a series of calls from the lake. At first I thought this was the strong song of a rare waterbird or other animal. It turned out to be Stefania's father, Fausto, hooting from the edge of his little boat. He was fishing for perch, to fry or pickle later with bay leaves. He appeared wild, more suited to a rushing river than the placid lake.

When we arrived at the large stone house, I was introduced to the entire living family. The younger children were in their pajamas, fresh and shiny after their baths. The parents and grandparents looked a little worn from another hot day with the land and the little ones. I met Giovanna that night. She was timid and slightly socially ticklish. It would take some coaxing for her to open up to the idea of us cooking together. It was determined that I should first cook with her sister-in-law Mariangela, and spend a few days with the whole family. Her brother, the feisty Fausto, would then give her his gruff nod of approval.

The next morning Giovanna and I took a stroll through the steeply sloped garden to gather chard and sage leaves for the buckwheat pasta, *pizzoccheri*, we were making with Mariangela. We passed rows and rows of greens and herbs, on land cultivated by her family for more than a century. Her relatives had been picking from the loquat tree for many generations, looking out at the same mountains that had folded themselves abruptly into Como's deep wide lake. She and Fausto were born, raised, and now growing old in this house. Her father was brought here with his younger siblings when his mother, an "excellent woman," died suddenly of the flu at age thirty-three. Giovanna's grandfather was away at the time, and did not hear of it for almost three weeks. His children came to Varenna to be raised by their aunts and grandmother, on this secluded land by the lake, where their ancestors had been living for as long as anyone could remember. This was a family that took care of one another amid and despite dire circumstances.

On our walk back to the house, we passed animal cages and fruit trees. There were chickens, parrots, and rabbits. The family's rabbits were all different shades of black and gray, and were exceptionally large. Apparently they didn't kill them very often, and when they did they chose an old male, or a female that had reproduced too many times and was growing tired. The women would snap the old rabbit's neck and then stew it, or make lean little sausages with its meat. This was an interesting place; the land appeared so calm and sheltered, yet there was something edgy about it. Perhaps it was

A view of Lake Como from my daily walk to Giovanna's house.

the lake's water, so soothing to the eye, but deceptively dark in its depths. Or the mountains, with their histories of death and hiding.

By the time Giovanna was ready to teach me her cooking, I knew exactly what I wanted to eat. The family members had each had their turn at telling me about her delicious food, their preferred savory dishes, and which of her weekly Sunday desserts was their favorite. Giovanna's cooking tended toward the sweet, yet always contained a hint of something unexpected—perhaps some bitter almonds or cacao, a squeeze of sour lemon, or a touch of salt to surprise. The pumpkin *tortelloni* were where I wanted to begin, and they were what she suggested for our first lunch together.

Giovanna had already roasted the green-skinned, orange-fleshed pumpkin by the time I arrived. We peeled off the pumpkin's skin, left on during the roasting to add richness and moisture, and pureed its flesh with a food mill. Little muscles popped out from Giovanna's long, sinewy arms with each turn of the blade. We crumbled *amaretti* cookies into the puree, for that touch of bittersweetness, and added a few eggs and Parmesan to bring the filling together. White pepper was sprinkled in, as it was milder and more floral than the dried black corns. And, as with almost all of her dishes, Giovanna grated in a touch of heady fresh nutmeg.

Giovanna preferred to make her own pasta. She liked the process, and it made the family so happy to eat the dishes she had made from scratch. After all, cooking was her "passion," and she took every opportunity she could to bring the family together over one of her passion-filled pastas or cakes. The dough she made that morning for the *tortelloni* was moist with eggs, worked well by hand but also by the pasta machine. She rolled it into extraordinarily long strips.

Giovanna had almost every cook's tool imaginable; for the *tortelloni*, she pulled out a special mold, soft cotton cloths, a very small rolling pin, a crinkled dough cutter, and cardboard trays to sprinkle with flour and store the tortelloni on before she boiled them. This was a woman who loved to cook, and had thought long and hard about how to be efficient and effective with her technique.

"This was a woman who loved to cook, and had thought long and hard about how to be efficient and effective with her technique."

Clockwise from top left: Giovanna's house. Giovanna rolls dough for her *Tortelloni di Zucca*. The cemetery passed on my daily walk to cook with Giovanna. Giovanna filling the *tortelloni* in her kitchen.

Something entirely unexpected happened that morning while Giovanna was filling the tortelloni. Half of the pasta strip had been laid down over the mold, and she was spooning the filling into the little holes. We were talking about pumpkins. Her family was particular about how they liked to eat them. Her granddaughter Lucrezia refused to eat them at all. Her son only liked them in the pumpkin *gnocchi* she made with a spoon. And the other family members each had a particular way they wanted to dress these dishes—a few with tomatoes, others with brown butter and herbs, and some with just a dusting of Parmesan. What about her husband, her son's father? That is what I asked, simply and innocently.

Giovanna's narrow hips flinched strongly, visibly. Then, slowly but fully, this reserved woman broke open. As a very young woman, Giovanna was impregnated out of wedlock. She gave birth to and kept her baby boy, and she and her family had raised him together. The details of the pregnancy were never talked about, and Giovanna and her son were simply absorbed into the existing family structure. Her son had never asked about his father, not once. Giovanna never married, and I'm not sure that it would have been possible; things were conservative during her youth, and it would have been very hard for a woman who already had a child to find a man to marry. She had lived with her parents her entire life, and still lived with her now ancient mother. She had raised a son, and was now raising her grandchildren, and had never really had an opportunity to leave home.

In the Italy of Giovanna's youth, if you got pregnant, you had the baby. I have been told that as an Italian woman, it is ideal to find yourself pregnant as the wife of a kind and wealthy man. In the worst-case scenario, the father of the child you are carrying is unknown, and after giving birth you drop your baby off at an orphanage. Anything and everything in between was possible, but you did not terminate the pregnancy. After all, this was the country where, in 1198, rotating wheels were installed outside foundling homes to allow for the deposit of unwanted babies. Too many dead infants had been found in the River Tiber before this system had provided an anonymous way of giving away one's child.

Giovanna's tears poured around, and I'm sure into, the sweet lumps of her soft pumpkin filling, as she told me about her youth, her pregnancy, her silence. I'm not sure if she had ever really told this story before. It was as if it had needed to escape for years, was handed to me quietly that day, and could be driven off in my leased Twingo car later in the week.

It was striking that at the beginning of our time together Giovanna had said that she didn't want her voice to be heard if I filmed her. That morning she spoke to me with such strength and courage that she seemed an entirely different woman from the one I had met just a few days earlier. I suppose we all need to tell our stories. So where are the best places for them to be cried or sung? Giovanna's love and grief were told to a stranger while she sweated over her daily passion. She did it in the safest and the fullest way she knew how, and I think it made a difference for both of us.

During my remaining days with Giovanna, there developed a closeness between us that took me by surprise. As we stirred milky bread for plum hearth cake and roasted more pumpkins, we shared our stories and confided in each other on matters of the heart. We spoke openly and at length about the differences between being a woman in Italy and America. I talked about my romantic uncertainties, the relationship I had left behind for the independence and adventure of Italy. Giovanna freely offered opinions on what she would do if it were her life, had she all the confidence and freedom in the world. To live for love was a great thing, and something she had always longed for. And yet, to travel around her great country, patiently gathering life's wisdom from the kitchen, was in her opinion a more thrilling opportunity. She strongly believed that what I would learn that year from the women and the food would be all my own, something to cherish closely and last me a lifetime.

When I finally left Giovanna to explore the kitchens around the Slow Food movement's headquarters in the Piedmont, it was a sad parting of newly dear friends. Despite Giovanna's initial reserve, she became one of my greatest allies in Italy. After my time with her, she faithfully called me every Sunday to make sure that I was okay, and to hear a report of my adventures. She had only been to the Emilia-Romagna region of Italy, and didn't like to go *in giro*; in her own life she didn't want to "get around" or "travel about." She preferred to hear about the distant hills and dishes of her country from me.

GIOVANNA : LAGO DI COMO, LOMBARDIA

Tortelloni di Zucca
(Pumpkin *Tortelloni* with Brown Butter and Sage)

Pizzoccheri alla Valtellinese
(Buckwheat Noodles with Cabbage, Potato, and Mountain Cheese)

Torta di Grigna
(Mountain Cocoa and Almond Cake)

La Miascia
(Bread and Milk Cake with Pears and Dried Plums)

Caramelized Orange-Chocolate Tart

Tortelloni di Zucca (Pumpkin *Tortelloni* with Brown Butter and Sage)
Serves 6

Unlike any other recipe I have come across for pumpkin *tortelloni*, Giovanna's calls for crumbled *amaretti* biscuits in the filling, which adds a hauntingly delicious bittersweetness to the dish. Although these *tortelloni* are traditionally made with an Italian pumpkin, I recommend using sweet winter squash in America, such as Kabocha, kuri, Hubbard, or butternut varieties. While not a requirement, if you like a smooth-textured filling, a food processor is helpful for pureeing the squash and grinding the *amaretti*.

For the pasta:
2⅔ cups type 00 flour
4 large eggs, at room temperature
1 tablespoon olive oil

1 large egg, whisked with a fork
¾ teaspoon salt
¼ teaspoon white pepper
Pinch of nutmeg

For the filling:
2 medium kabocha squash, dry-roasted
   at 400 degrees F until soft
¼ cup finely grated Parmesan
6 tablespoons ground amaretti biscuits
   (crushed by hand or processed in a
   food processor)

For the brown butter and sage:
½ cup unsalted butter
6–8 sage leaves
1 teaspoon lemon juice
½ cup finely grated Parmesan
Salt

To prepare the pasta, clean a breadboard or countertop well, and dust it lightly with flour. Measure the flour into a large bowl and make a well in the center of it. Add the eggs and olive oil. Using a fork or your fingers, scramble the eggs together, slowly incorporating the flour until the dough has become a shaggy mass. Feel free to add a sprinkling of water if the dough is having a very hard time coming together. Turn the dough onto your clean board and knead it until it is smooth and pliant, 5 to 10 minutes. The dough is ready when it rebounds to the press of a thumb. Cover closely with a clean cloth (or plastic wrap) and set aside for 30 minutes to rest.

While the pasta dough rests, prepare the filling. Scoop out 2 cups of roasted squash into a bowl, reserving the rest for another use. Puree the squash in a food processor for a smoother filling, or mash by hand. Add the remaining filling ingredients to the puree and stir to combine.

After the dough has rested for 30 minutes, cut it into eight pieces of equal size. Press down on each piece of dough to flatten it slightly, and then roll it out on the widest setting of a pasta machine. One you have passed a piece of dough through once, fold it into thirds and pass it through again. Do this a couple of times for each piece of dough, dusting lightly with flour before each pass through the rollers if the dough is a bit sticky. This procedure will not only condition the dough but also form pieces that are roughly the width of the pasta rollers, producing the ideal size for filling the pasta later on. In between rollings, place the pasta on clean cloths that have been lightly dusted with flour. If you find that the rolling is taking a long time, cover the pasta with cloths to prevent the sheets from drying out.

After rolling the dough through the first setting a couple of times, adjust the pasta machine to the next (smaller-sized, larger-numbered) hole and pass each piece of dough through this setting. Continue this process, increasing the settings incrementally until you reach number 5. When you get to number 5, pass each piece of dough through twice, resulting in 8 pasta sheets measuring 16 by 4 inches each.

On the lower half of a pasta sheet, place 1 tablespoon of filling every 2 inches just above the center of the sheet. Fold the top half of the pasta sheet over the filled half. Press down around the edges of the filling to remove any air bubbles and seal the filling in. If you have a water mister, lightly spray the pasta before folding it over; this is an easy way to create a good seal. Cut the pasta into individual *tortelloni* with a zigzag cutter or knife. Repeat this procedure until you run out of the pasta or filling. Place the *tortelloni* on a well-floured sheet pan, so that they aren't touching. If you won't be cooking them immediately, cover and refrigerate.

Put a large pot of salted water on the stove to a boil. Meanwhile, in a saute pan, prepare the brown butter and sage sauce by melting the butter over low heat until the foam subsides and it becomes golden brown in color. Add the sage leaves, turning them every few seconds. When the butter turns tawny brown, remove the pan from the heat and add the lemon juice. The sage leaves should become nice and crispy during their brief cook in the butter; if at any point they appear close to burning, strain them out with a fork and store them on a paper towel for the final pasta.

Boil the *tortelloni* for 5 to 10 minutes, depending on how long you stored them before cooking. Freshly made *tortelloni* will cook more quickly than those that have been refrigerated. Drain the *tortelloni*, reserving ½ cup pasta water, and return the *tortelloni* to the pot. Pour over the brown butter and sage, moistening if necessary with the pasta water. Serve immediately, sprinkled with freshly grated Parmesan cheese.

Pizzoccheri alla Valtellinese

Serves 4 as an entrée, 6 as an appetizer

Pizzoccheri is one of my favorite things to eat. It is an earthy, creamy mess of buckwheat pasta, greens, and cheese, designed to delight the child in us. Giovanna, and I cooked it as a one-pot dish, boiling the pasta and other ingredients all together, then tossing them with butter and sage and stinky cheese at the end. After talking with Giovanna about the recipe, however, I decided to develop it further to better articulate the strengths of the dish. I make the noodles slightly thicker and stouter, boil the vegetables separately so as not to overcook them, and broil the dish at the end for a slightly crunchy and caramelized top. If you do not have time to make the fresh buckwheat pasta for this recipe, you can substitute 8 to 12 ounces of dried buckwheat noodles.

For the buckwheat pasta:
1⅓ cups buckwheat flour
1 cup type 00 flour, or all-purpose flour
3 large eggs, at room temperature
1 tablespoon whole milk
Pinch of salt

For the *pizzoccheri* vegetables:
2–3 medium Yukon Gold potatoes, peeled
  and diced in ½" cubes (roughly 1½ cups)
2 cup shredded Swiss chard, stems removed
3 cups shredded savoy or green cabbage
½ cup (1 stick) butter
4 cloves garlic, peeled and smashed
8 fresh sage leaves
⅓ cup pasta cooking water, divided
Salt
1 cup Taleggio cheese cut in ¼" cubes
1 cup freshly grated Parmesan
1 teaspoon white or black pepper

To prepare the buckwheat pasta, place the two flours in a large bowl and mix together with a wooden spoon. Make a well in the middle of the flour; into the well crack the eggs, pour the milk, and sprinkle the salt. Using a fork or your fingers, scramble the eggs and milk together, slowly incorporating the flour until the dough has become a rough, shaggy mass.

Turn the dough onto a clean, lightly floured surface, and knead it with a fair amount of energy and weight for 15 to 20 minutes. Remember to dust the surface with flour from time to time, kneading until you have a firm but elastic dough. Wrap in a clean cloth or plastic wrap, and let the dough rest for 30 minutes.

Divide the dough into three parts and roll it out in a pasta machine, beginning at the widest setting. Pass it through the widest setting a few times, folding the rolled pieces into thirds each time (as if you were folding a piece of paper to put it in an envelope) and passing through again. Once you have done this two or three times for each piece of dough, adjust the machine to the next hole (number 2). Pass each piece of dough one time through each of the settings on the machine until you reach the second to last setting, number 5.

After you have passed each piece of dough through the number 5 setting, cut the pasta sheets crosswise into strips 3 inches long and about ¾ inch wide. Sprinkle the cut noodles lightly with flour, and set aside to wait for cooking until the other ingredients for the *pizzoccheri* are ready for assembly.

To prepare the vegetables for the *pizzoccheri*, preheat the broiler in your oven, or turn the oven as high as it can go.

Bring a large pot of water to a boil, and salt it generously. Boil the potatoes until tender, about 7 minutes, and remove with a slotted spoon. In the same water, blanch the chard and cabbage for about 2 minutes, and remove with a slotted spoon. Finally, boil the fresh pasta in the same water until *al dente*, about 2 minutes.

While the pasta is cooking, place the butter, garlic cloves, sage leaves, and ¼ cup of the pasta water in a large, wide nonreactive pan. Melt slowly over low heat, swirling the butter and water into a sauce and stirring frequently; do not boil. After a few minutes, discard the garlic and shut off the heat. Salt lightly, to taste.

When the pasta is *al dente*, add the potatoes and cabbage back into the boiling water for a second to briefly reheat. Drain the pot into a colander, reserving a small amount of pasta water. Add the pasta and vegetables to the pan with butter sauce, and toss to coat. There should be slightly more than enough sauce to coat it all; if not, add a little of the extra pasta water to loosen it up. Finally, add all of the Taleggio and ½ cup of the Parmesan to the pan; toss once or twice, only enough to mix. Scoop everything into an ovenproof dish. Top the pasta with the remaining ½ cup Parmesan and broil until the cheese is melted and begins to brown on top, about 2 minutes. Serve with freshly ground black or white pepper.

Optional: Though it is not traditional, adding 1 teaspoon fresh lemon juice to the pasta and vegetables, along with the butter sauce, lightens the final pasta.

Torta di Grigna (Mountain Cocoa and Almond Cake)

Makes a 9-inch cake

Named after the highest mountain of Lake Como, Grigna, this tall cake takes after its namesake in both height and heft. Legend has it that the cake was first made by the residents of Mandello, where there is a good view of the mountain. In this adapted version of the well-established recipe, cream is added to contribute moisture and a richer crumb.

1¼ cups (2½ sticks) unsalted butter, softened	2 cups all-purpose flour, sifted
1½ cups sugar	2 tablespoons cocoa powder, sifted
5 large eggs, separated	2 teaspoons baking powder
¾ cup heavy cream (milk will also do)	1 teaspoon baking soda
1 cup raw almonds	Small pinch of salt

Preheat your oven to 350 degrees F. Butter and sugar a 9-inch round cake pan (preferably a springform pan).

Cream together the soft butter and sugar, using an electric mixer or the vigorous beating of a wooden spoon. Add the egg yolks and the cream, and continue to mix until thoroughly combined. Chop the almonds into small pieces, and add ½ cup of them to the bowl along with the flour, cocoa powder, baking powder, baking soda, and salt. Thoroughly mix the batter, this time using a wooden spoon. This cake batter is a very stiff one, requiring a fair amount of muscular effort to combine the ingredients; do not be alarmed, but proceed ahead with confidence and vigor.

Whip the egg whites until they form soft peaks, and add them to the batter. Mix them in thoroughly with your wooden spoon; you will need to beat rather strongly to incorporate them. Again, this is normal for this cake.

Spoon your thick batter into the prepared cake pan, spreading it out evenly. Finally, sprinkle the top of the cake with the remaining ½ cup chopped almonds. The cake will bake for 1 to 1¼ hours. Begin to check on it after 50 minutes, and then again every 10 minutes; it's done with the middle-top of the cake no longer jiggles to the touch, and a toothpick inserted in the center comes out clean. At this point the edges of the cake will have slightly pulled away from the sides of the pan.

Remove from the oven and set aside to cool thoroughly before serving.

La Miascia (Bread and Milk Cake with Pears and Dried Plums)

Makes a 9-inch cake

La Miascia is the poor-man's cake of Lake Como, making delicious use of those things that one might otherwise find undesirable. According to Giovanna, there is no recipe for *La Miascia*, it being an impromptu dessert that the thrifty housewife pulls together from old bread, overly ripe fruit, and some fresh milk, and then bakes in the glowing embers of her hearth. This cake is a shock and delight to make; from stale bread, *La Miascia* transforms itself into a creamy, moist cake with a slightly crunchy top. It is wonderful served warm, eaten in the afternoon with tea, or as a soft and sweet breakfast.

11 ounces dry old bread (see note below)
2 cups whole milk
2 medium ripe pears
3 tablespoons sultanas or raisins, soaked in
  warm water to plump
4 dried plums or prunes, thinly sliced
3 dried figs, thinly sliced
1 lemon, zested and juiced
3 large eggs
½ cup plus 1 tablespoon sugar, divided
¼ cup (½ stick) butter, melted, divided
Pinch of salt
Fresh nutmeg

Note: This recipe makes use of old bread that is too stale to enjoy as part of the normal course of a meal. The recipe is best when made with a plain artisan-style loaf—one that is not sour and contains no seeds or nuts. If you prepare the bread specifically for this recipe (rather than just using leftover old bread), cut off the crust, slice the loaf into thick pieces, and leave them out to dry for 2 to 3 days. You will need 11 ounces of crustless dry bread, about 1 loaf's worth.

Preheat your oven to 350 degrees F. Butter and sugar a 9-inch round cake pan.

Break the bread into small pieces, place them in a large bowl, and pour the milk over them. Set aside for an hour or more, turning the bread in the milk from time to time and crushing it with

your hands. Soak the bread until it has broken down into a homogeneous mass of moist shreds. There should be no loose milk remaining once the bread has broken down; if there is excess, strain it off and discard.

Peel and core the pears, and cut them into small rough pieces. Add to the soft bread. Strain the raisins of their excess liquid and add them to the bread along with the sliced dried plums and figs. Add the lemon zest and 1 tablespoon of lemon juice. Gently mix together with your hands or a spoon.

Whisk together the eggs, ½ cup of the sugar, 3 tablespoons of the melted butter, and a pinch of salt. Gently fold this into the bread-and-fruit mixture.

Pour the mixture into your prepared cake pan. Dust the surface of the cake with freshly grated nutmeg, Drizzle or brush with the remaining tablespoon of melted butter, and sprinkle the top of the cake with the remaining tablespoon of sugar.

Bake for 1¼ hours. Turn the heat up to 375 degrees F and bake for an additional 15 minutes to lightly brown the top of the cake. *La Miascia* is done when its top is a slightly crunchy medium golden brown, and the cake has pulled away from the sides of the pan.

Caramelized Orange-Chocolate Tart

Makes a 9-inch tart

The refined elegance and sweetness of this tart epitomize all that Giovanna represented to me. Here, a sweet pastry crust is filled with a simple chocolate ganache, then topped with caramelized slices of slowly cooked citrus fruit. I prefer to use a combination of tangerines, clementines, and kumquats, but whole oranges also work very well. This tart is the perfect rich, wintertime dessert.

For the tart shell:
1¼ cups flour
⅔ cup powdered sugar
A pinch of salt
½ cup (1 stick) frozen butter, cut into ½-inch cubes
1 large egg yolk
1 tablespoon plus ½ teaspoon heavy cream
Extra flour, for dusting (about 1 tablespoon)

For the caramelized oranges:
1 pound organic tangerines, kumquats, or oranges
⅔ cup water
⅓ cup sugar

For the chocolate filling:
1 pound 70% cocoa content chocolate
1½ cups heavy cream
½ teaspoon ground cinnamon
6 tablespoons (¾ stick) unsalted butter, cut into pieces

To make the tart shell, whisk together the flour, sugar, and salt in a large bowl. Cut in the butter using a pastry cutter until the mixture resembles coarse sand (you can also do this in a food processor by pulsing in the butter in short bursts). In a small bowl, whisk together the egg yolk and cream; add to the dry ingredients, mixing and pressing with your hands just enough to bring the dough together. Press into a flat disk and wrap tightly in plastic wrap. Refrigerate for about 2 hours, until the dough is hard enough to roll without sticking.

Lightly flour a clean surface or piece of parchment paper. Roll the dough into a circle about

⅛ inch thick. Make sure to turn the dough during the rolling, scraping underneath with a large knife if necessary to keep it from sticking. Feel free to add up to a total of 1 tablespoon of flour while rolling; however, if the dough becomes soft, stop rolling and place it in the refrigerator again until it hardens back up.

Roll the dough loosely over the rolling pin and unfurl it over a 9-inch fluted tart pan. Lift up the edges of the dough, then settle and press it down into the edges of the pan to make a ¼-inch border. Cut a clean edge along the sides of the pan by rolling the pin over the sides or trimming with a sharp knife. Gently prick the bottom of the tart in a number of places with the tines of a fork. Place in the refrigerator for at least another 30 minutes to chill.

Preheat the oven to 375 degrees F. Line the tart with foil, and fill with pie weights or old beans. Bake the tart shell on top of a baking sheet for 30 minutes, turning the pan halfway through baking. After 30 minutes, remove the foil and weights, and return the tart shell to the oven. Bake for a further 5 to 10 minutes, until the shell is lightly browned. Set aside to cool.

Wash the citrus fruits well, and thoroughly dry them. Using a very sharp knife, slice the citrus crosswise into very thin rounds. Discard the ends. Lay the slices in a 9-by-13-inch baking dish, and sprinkle with the water and sugar. Cover with foil and bake at 325 degrees F for 60 to 75 minutes, until the peels of the fruits are tender.

Turn the oven up to 400 degrees F. Uncover the dish and bake for an additional 10 to 15 minutes, until the citrus has become sticky and the juices thick and syrupy. Set aside to cool. I prefer to prepare the oranges the same day that I make the tart, as they remain soft and cut easily with the tart. For a firmer orange, however, they can be stored in the fridge for 3 to 4 days prior to assembling the tart.

To prepare the chocolate filling, chop the chocolate into small pieces, and place in a medium-size mixing bowl. Warm the cream over medium-high heat until it starts to give off steam and looks close to a boil. Turn off the heat at this point; pour the hot cream over the chocolate, and sprinkle on the cinnamon. Stir thoroughly to combine. Add the butter, and gently stir to incorporate. Pour the chocolate filling into the cooled tart shell, and set aside to allow the chocolate to set up. Garnish with the oranges, and place the tart in the refrigerator to finish solidifying, 1 to 2 hours.

Irene

Per capire una cosa, devi guardare alle radici.

To understand something, you must look at its roots.

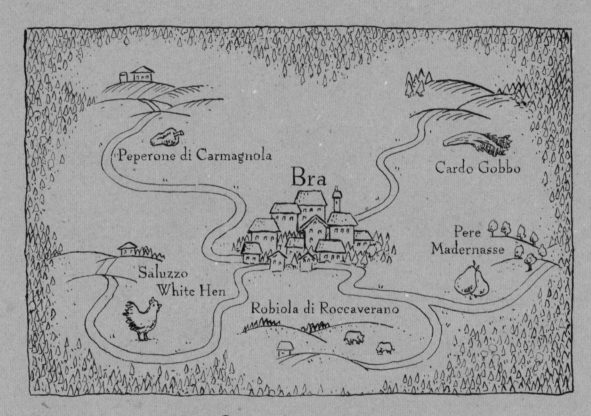

Peperone di Carmagnola

Cardo Gobbo

Bra

Pere Madernasse

Saluzzo White Hen

Robiola di Roccaverano

Bra, Piemonte

Upon arriving in the Piedmontese town of Bra one foggy October evening, I had the immediate impression that too many cars had passed too many times through its narrow streets, leaving their mark with exhaust fumes on walls and in lungs. This came with some surprise. As home to the international headquarters of the Slow Food movement, Bra was a much-anticipated destination on my travels. I had hardly expected it to feel so grimy and worn. From the time I'd first read about Slow Food, some years earlier, I'd been captivated. The organization was founded in Italy in 1989 to counteract the trend toward fast food and a faster life. It promoted the values of traditional foods and their preparation, the pleasures of the table, of conviviality, and of a life lived in connection to one's local terrain.

Cooking with Italy's grandmothers and learning their traditions was kindred to Slow Food's mission, and my journey had been largely inspired by the group. Before leaving the United States I had e-mailed their general address to inquire about visiting Slow Food's base in Bra. I outlined the details of my project and hoped for a response. Almost immediately a man named Carlo Fanti e-mailed me back in English. He thought my ideas were interesting and was happy to introduce me to many of the farmers involved in Slow Food's Presidia Project—a program created to support the continuation of delicious but endangered foods, and their producers. Carlo even offered to arrange for me to stay and cook with his friend Irene when I came to Bra. I gladly accepted.

When I arrived at Irene's door, a strapping young man answered the door: Stephano, Irene's youngest son. He showed me to my room, gave me a key to the house, and told me to go and have dinner at Boccondivino, Slow Food's *osteria* in town. That evening in Bra, I had my first *panna cotta* ever, my first taste of silk for the mouth. That *panna cotta* changed how I think about cooked cream desserts; it also became my mark of a good restaurant for the rest of my time in Italy.

Each morning for the next few weeks I went downstairs in my red terry-cloth bathrobe to be greeted by Irene and the roar of her little stovetop *espresso* maker. We would talk about the day's plans, our shared interest in psychology, the history of various Piedmontese foods, and what we could cook together that evening. We ate whole-grain sourdough bread slathered with the loose, sticky jams Irene made each summer. My favorite was the slightly sour apricot, which had a tendency to drip right off the bread if you tilted the slice too far to one side.

Irene seemed to know about everything. She had been a literature teacher for years, and was now beginning to work in local politics and training to become a Gestalt psychotherapist. There was always classical music playing in her home library, and talk of local history at her table. She was the most grounded, intellectual, and emotionally intelligent woman I knew. And she cooked in a way that made me feel as though everything in the world was going to be okay.

My days in Bra were filled with curiosity and learning. With Carlo as my guide, I traveled from farm to farm, meeting and spending time with the Presidia producers. By the afternoon I would eagerly return home, and Irene and I would make dinner together with the ingredients she had bought and those I'd gathered from the farmers.

Perhaps the most intriguing item I brought home to cook with Irene was the *cardo gobbo*, the hunchback cardoon. The most famous dish of the Langhe, *bagna cauda*, revolves around this cardoon; it is the most fitting variety of vegetable to dip into the hot, garlic-anchovy sauce. I had driven my Twingo through the rain one day to meet a Presidia farmer named Claudio Vaccaneo and learn about his rare cardoons.

During the first part of its cultivation, the *cardo gobbo* looks like many other cardoons—upright, bright green, and leafy, almost like an artichoke plant. And then something drastic happens: One by one, the farmer digs holes alongside the rows of growing cardoons. He then bends the cardoons over, being careful not to cut their roots, and buries them in the sandy, breathable dirt. The cardoons finish their growth underground, where they lose their chlorophyll and bitterness, becoming white and crunchy. Unlike other cardoons, the hunchbacks are suitable to be eaten raw, dipped into the pungent *bagna cauda*.

The *cardo gobbo* was an amazing plant, with a fascinating history and connection to local cuisine. It was the perfect example of a successful Presidia project—only the soils of Nizza were suitable for growing it, and all the labor had to be done by hand. Slow Food had created a viable

Nuns on the streets of Bra.

market for the hunchback cardoon, and as a result not only did the variety survive, but the traditional way of eating *bagna cauda* was ensured, as well.

That night, while preparing the *bagna cauda* and talking about the dish's origins, Irene said something very simple and profound that struck a deep chord of truth in me. She said that in order to understand something, you must look at its roots. To really know something deeply, you must become familiar with how it is born. This was clearly true for the *bagna cauda*; to understand it fully, one must uncover its origins, which lay not only in the cardoon, but also the Ligurian-Piedmontese trade routes by which salt and anchovies were brought to the Langhe from the Ligurian coast. Upon further reflection, what was true for a dish also appeared to be true for almost everything in life.

The Piedmontese vegetables I discovered with Irene were as earthy as she was. Around the hills of the Langhe one could find pungent cabbage of all sorts, vibrant and intense peppers, hazelnuts, and turnips. Together we chopped red cabbage and sautéed it with apples and onions to bring out the leaves' innate sweetness, adding plenty of red wine to loosen things up when the pan got sticky. We boiled the bitter outer leaves of *puntarella* greens, then thinly sliced and deeply chilled their inner hearts. Irene believed in cooking these ingredients with simplicity, in keeping herself out of the way of their natural flavors and allowing the essence of the foods to shine. She brought a similar approach to conversation, listening much more than she spoke; asking questions more often than she answered them. Her questions were always important and precise, and ignited deep reflection. At the end of each evening spent cooking and talking with Irene, I always found I had learned as much about myself as I had about the ingredients we had worked with.

Mealtime at Irene's symbolized what I saw to be her approach to life: You welcome whatever arrives, and then you listen closely and nourish well. On Sundays, family and friends would appear for the midday meal, and they would often join us for our regular post-lunch stroll. On one particular Sunday we decided to take a very long walk through the hills and castle towns of the Langhe. The afternoon ahead of us called for a substantial meal: polenta with Bra's special veal sausages, and slowly cooked *peperoni di Carmagnola*, a fleshy local Presidia pepper.

Irene knew that the thick, meaty *Carmagnola* peppers would be sweeter now that we were at the end of their season. It was amazing to me that one could have lived in a town for long enough to know when a particular type of pepper would be the sweetest, or when its skin was the toughest, and the ways in which the textures and flavors of the pepper could be complimented by one's cooking methods.

"Mealtime at Irene's symbolized what I saw to be her approach to life: You welcome whatever arrives, and then you listen closely and nourish well."

Irene at her kitchen table.

As Irene cooked the locally grown, stone-ground *polenta* for the meal, she told me something new about the ubiquitous coarse cornmeal: that an old nickname for Northern Italians was *polentone*, or "big polentas." Corn for *polenta* in Italy had always been grown in the lowlands of the Po valley, an area that runs about four hundred miles east to west, from the Alps to the Adriatic. Thus, *polenta* eaters had traditionally been northerners and came to be referred to by the name of one of their staple foods.

At the end of the meal we nibbled on slices of creamy Robiola as Irene described the origins of that cheese. There had been incredible poverty throughout steep hills of the Langhe during times past. With their spare time, and any leftover milk from their cows, sheep, and goats, the local women would gather together and make the Robiola. They would age the creamy squares until their soft rinds just started to bloom, and then bring them to market to sell. Together the women had enough milk to do this, and it was yet another example of how Italian women had worked cooperatively over the centuries to turn food into both nourishment and profit.

Cooking with Irene, I gained a tangible sense of all the labor and history that has traditionally gone into making meals. There was the earth and her farmers, the sea and the fishermen, the people who transported the food, the market sellers, the home cooks, and there was Slow Food and the Presidia producers, ensuring that the most unlikely and rare foods could still find their way to the table. Often it takes a whole community to ensure the preservation of those things that are the most valuable and dear to us. Bra was a beautiful example of this idea in action.

IRENE : BRA, PIEMONTE

MENU ONE

Bagna Cauda
  (Piedmontese Warm Garlic-Anchovy Dip)

Gnocchi di Semola
  (Semolina Flour *Gnocchi*)

Insalate di Puntarella
  (*Puntarella* Salad, Inside and Out)

Pere Madernasse con Mandorle e Prugne
  (Caramel-Poached Pears with Prunes, Almonds, and Cream)

MENU TWO

Lentil Soup with Turnips and Pounded Walnuts

Cavolo Rosso
  (Sweet-and-Sour Red Cabbage)

Panna Cotta with Wine Syrup

Paste di Meliga
  (Piedmontese Cornmeal Biscuits)

Menu One

Bagna Cauda (Piedmontese Warm Garlic-Anchovy Dip)
Serves 6 as an appetizer

Irene's version of *bagna cauda*—a traditional dip served throughout the Langhe during autumn months—is my favorite of all those I've tried. Irene boils her garlic in water before adding it to the warm olive oil, which makes for a much smoother taste than recipes that call for raw garlic. *Bagna cauda* is believed to be the dish of friendship, best eaten by candlelight with one's family and friends on a cold evening.

3 whole heads garlic, broken into cloves and peeled
⅔–1 cup olive oil, depending on how thick you like the dip
5 oil- or salt-cured anchovy fillets, rinsed if salted, and finely minced
4 stalks cardoon
2 bulbs fennel
3 large colored peppers
Freshly cracked black pepper
Salt to taste

Boil the peeled garlic cloves in water for 10 minutes. Strain the garlic cloves from the water, and mash them—through a garlic press or potato ricer, by mortar and pestle, or by hand. Warm the olive oil in a terra-cotta or other nonreactive pot set over very low heat. Add the anchovies and mashed garlic, and simmer very gently for half an hour.

Prepare the vegetables for the dish while the *bagna cauda* is simmering. De-fiber the stalks of cardoon by peeling them in the same way you would a stalk of celery, then cut them into batons and simmer in water until slightly softened, about 10 minutes (you can use the garlic water for this if you like). Slice off the very bottoms of the fennel bulbs, then slice them lengthwise into slabs about a ¼ inch thick. Tear the peppers into large bite-size pieces. Arrange the vegetables on a platter.

Before serving the *bagna cauda*, add black pepper to taste, and salt if the anchovies have not provided enough. Ideally, the *bagna cauda* should be served warm; in the Piedmont a burning candle is placed under the terra-cotta dish to keep the dip warm during eating.

Gnocchi di Semola (Semolina Flour *Gnocchi*)
Serves 4 as a main course, 6–8 as a starter

I was shocked to watch Irene make these ancient *gnocchi* on my first Sunday in Bra; until that moment I had only known *gnocchi* to be a potato-based dish. In keeping with the dish's Roman roots, Irene makes hers from coarsely ground semolina flour, hot milk, and eggs. To form the *gnocchi*, a rich *polenta*-like paste is prepared, cooled, and then cut into disks using the wet rim of a small glass. The disks are then sprinkled with Parmesan and bread crumbs, and baked in a hot oven to puff them up.

1 quart milk
2–3 teaspoons salt
7 ounces semolina flour (just over 1 cup)
1 cup finely grated Parmesan cheese, divided
2 large eggs, lightly beaten
1 tablespoon butter
½ cup bread crumbs

Heat the milk and salt in a medium saucepan set over medium heat. When the milk starts to simmer, slowly sprinkle in the semolina flour, whisking constantly to make sure that lumps do not form. Once all the flour has been added, reduce the heat to medium-low. Continue to whisk for 7 to 10 more minutes, until the batter has become thick and velvety.

Remove the pan from the heat and stir in ½ cup of the Parmesan, the eggs, and the butter. Pour the batter into a large, shallow baking dish, spreading it out to make a layer of even thickness (roughly ½ an inch high). Set aside (in the fridge if there is room) for about an hour, to cool and become firm.

Cut the semolina into *gnocchi* using the mouth of a glass about 2 inches wide, or a cookie cutter. Dip the glass into water between each press to prevent the dough from sticking. Lay the *gnocchi* on a parchment-paper-lined baking sheet, making sure to leave at least ½ inch between them so that their edges can completely caramelize.

Sprinkle the tops of the gnocchi with the remaining ½ cup Parmesan and the bread crumbs. Bake at 400 degrees F until golden brown, slightly puffed, and crispy around the edges, 30 to 40 minutes.

Insalate di Puntarella
(*Puntarella* Salad, Inside and Out)
Serves 4 as a side dish

Irene has great appreciation for Roman cuisine, mostly because it makes good use of unusual vegetables such as the *puntarella*—a large, leafy green chicory. It has dark serrated leaves, which are bitter in taste, similar to dandelion greens. What makes the *puntarella* particularly special is that hidden deep within its leaves often lies a heart of sweet, crunchy shoots. This is of exceptional delight to Irene, as it allows for two types of salad to be prepared from a single vegetable.

In these recipes the bitter outer *puntarella* leaves, although traditionally boiled, are steam-sautéed with a little oil and garlic, and garnished with lemon and toasted walnuts. The pale green shoots are cut lengthwise into thin strips and soaked in ice water, prompting them to curl slightly into beautiful spirals. These crunchy shoots are eaten with a pungent dressing made from anchovies, olive oil, and a touch of raw garlic. Irene thinks of this salad as a cold, springtime version of *bagna cauda*. If you cannot find *puntarella*, feel free to substitute dandelion greens in the cooked salad.

For the outer-leaf cooked salad:
1 pound leaves, from 1–2 puntarelle
2 tablespoons olive oil
2 cloves garlic, finely slivered
½–¾ teaspoon salt
½ lemon

For the garnish:
1 tablespoon olive oil
3 tablespoons chopped toasted walnuts

Cut the greens crosswise in half and wash well. Place them directly into a large pot without drying. Add the olive oil, garlic, and salt. Cook over low heat, covered with a lid, for 10 minutes. Take off the lid, turn up the heat to medium-low, and cook uncovered for 10 minutes more. Make sure to stir the greens every couple of minutes. They're done when the moisture has evaporated and they've become shiny and sticky. Right at the end of cooking, add the lemon juice, give the greens another stir, and turn off the heat. Serve warm or at room temperature, with a drizzle of olive oil and scattering of chopped walnuts.

For the chilled salad of inner buds:
¼ pound inner hearts of puntarella
Juice of ½ lemon
½ small clove garlic, very finely minced
2 oil- or salt-cured anchovies
1 teaspoon fresh lemon juice
1 tablespoon olive oil
⅛ teaspoon salt

For the garnish:
1 tablespoon chopped parsley
1–2 ounces Parmesan cheese

Cut the *puntarella* tips into individual fingers, and then slice them lengthwise, as thinly as you possibly can. Press the *puntarella* fingers flat as you cut them, slightly crushing them to break their fibers—this will make them curl more easily as they chill. Immediately after cutting, place the long strips into an ice-and-water bath into which half a lemon has been squeezed; the lemon prevents them from browning, and the ice makes them curl.

Once you have sliced all the tips, chill them for about 1 to 2 hours in the ice bath, until the strips have started to gently curl. Strain from the ice and dry well.

While the *puntarella* ribbons are chilling, make the dressing. Press the finely minced garlic into a paste by sprinkling it with a little salt and crushing it with the back of a large knife. Finely mince the anchovies, and then also crush them into paste with the back of the knife. Place the garlic and anchovies in a bowl. Whisk in the lemon juice, olive oil, and salt.

Immediately before serving, toss the chilled *puntarella* ribbons with the dressing and parsley. Finish by shaving wide ribbons of Parmesan over the top of the *puntarella* with a vegetable peeler.

Pere Madernasse con Mandorle e Prugne
(Caramel-Poached Pears with Prunes, Almonds, and Cream)
Serves 6–8

While I was living with Irene, she made a number of dishes with *La Madernassa*, the Piedmont's ancient and beloved cooking pear. She began with the most typical way of preparing the pears: *Pere al Vino*, pears poached in local red wine with sugar and cinnamon. While these were delicious, it was her caramel-poached pears that I found most memorable. To make these pears, you prepare a caramel and then add the pears to it, covering the pot with a lid and cooking it over exceptionally low heat for a long time. Even if the caramel remains hard during much of the cooking, it slowly softens, giving way to a pear-infused caramel sauce by the time the pears have cooked. For this dish, it is important to use a hard cooking pear, such as the Bosc.

> *1¼ cups sugar*
> *Juice of 1 lemon*
> *6 hard cooking pears, cored, peeled, and quartered*
> *1 cup whole prunes*
> *1 cup whole raw almonds*
> *¾ cup heavy cream*

Slowly melt the sugar and lemon juice together over low heat in a large, heavy-bottomed pot or saucepan. Do not stir the mixture, as it will clump and stick; instead, swirl the pan to distribute the melting sugar.

Once the sugar has completely melted and turned a golden brown, add the pears, cover the pot, and turn the heat down to very low (as low as you can get the flame). Cook covered for about 1 hour, turning the pears a couple of times.

After an hour, add the prunes and almonds, and stir to combine. Re-cover the pan and cook for another 20 minutes, until the pears have softened and the prunes and raisins have plumped up.

Whip the cream to very soft peaks. Serve the pears warm with a large spoonful of the unsweetened whipped cream.

Menu Two

Lentil Soup with Turnips and Pounded Walnuts
Serves 4–6

One of the things that I most appreciated about Irene's cooking was her tendency toward healthy preparations; in addition to using lots of unusual vegetables, her dinners often included a variety of whole grains and legumes. This soup is based on one that she made for me with the unusual, yellow-fleshed *Caprauna* turnips, another Slow Food Presidia product. The soup relies on the use of tiny lentils; both puy and beluga black lentils would be good choices here. If possible, make the dish with fresh herbs, and be sure to include the pounded walnuts as a garnish. This is a soup that is best prepared ahead of time; after sitting for a couple of hours the flavors come together and the soup thickens to the desired consistency.

4 cloves garlic, finely minced
2 teaspoons finely minced fresh savory,
  or 1½ teaspoons finely crumbled dried savory
2 teaspoons finely minced fresh marjoram,
  or 1½ teaspoons dried
2 teaspoons fresh thyme leaves,
  or 1 teaspoon dried
½ small dried hot pepper, minced
¼ cup olive oil
1½ cups very small lentils, sorted and washed
½ cup white wine
5½ cups water
1½ cups turnips, medium dice
1 teaspoon salt

For the garnish:
⅓ cup fresh walnuts, pounded in a pestle and
  mortar or with the back of a knife
Olive oil
1 tablespoon chopped parsley

In a medium pot set over medium heat, slowly sauté the garlic, savory, marjoram, thyme leaves, and hot pepper in the olive oil. Sauté for about 3 minutes, until the garlic starts to turn a golden brown. Add the lentils and sauté them also for a few minutes, to evaporate the water and coat them in the oil and herbs. When the lentils start to crackle a bit, add the white wine and stir well. Add the water and bring to a simmer.

Partially cover the pot with a lid, bring to a strong simmer, and cook over medium heat for 40 minutes. Add the turnips and salt, and simmer for 20 to 25 minutes more, until the lentils and turnips have softened and the soup has thickened.

Serve garnished with a generous sprinkling of pounded walnuts, a healthy drizzle of olive oil, and a sprinkling of parsley.

Cavolo Rosso (Sweet-and-Sour Red Cabbage)

Serves 4–6 as a side dish

Irene is known far and wide for her wine-flavored red cabbage. She subtly sweetens it through slowly cooking it with heirloom apples and caramelized red onions; acidity is added through the region's hearty red wine. This dish makes perfect use of one's leftover wine, and pairs beautifully with many of Irene's other dishes.

2 small red onions, thinly sliced (1½ cups)
2 tablespoons olive oil
3 cloves garlic, minced
1 red cabbage (about 2 pounds), cored and cut into ¼" slices
1 large sweet apple, cored and cut into thin wedges
¾ cup hearty red wine
1¼ teaspoons salt

In a large sauté pan set over medium heat, cook the red onions in the olive oil with a pinch of salt. Sauté until golden and slightly softened, 7 to 10 minutes. Add the garlic, then the cabbage and apple, stirring well to combine. Cook uncovered for about 5 minutes, until the cabbage and apple begin to caramelize. Add the red wine and salt, bring to a gentle simmer, and cover the pan. Slowly cook for about 45 minutes, stirring from time to time. The cabbage and apples are done when they are tender through, but still holding their form.

Panna Cotta with Wine Syrup

Serves 6–8

Upon tasting Boccondivino's perfect *panna cotta* in Bra, my standards for the dessert were set. After months of experimenting to find the exact portions and technique that would replicate that creamy taste of silk for the mouth, I arrived at this recipe. The wine syrup makes the dessert distinctly Piedmontese. However, there are many ways to accompany *panna cotta*, and my favorites include: cherries and caramel sauce in summer, fresh strawberries in spring, and warm chocolate sauce with caramelized nuts during wintertime.

1 cup whole milk
3 cups heavy cream
2¾ teaspoons gelatin
Tiny pinch of fine salt
6 tablespoons sugar
½ vanilla bean, slit lengthwise with paring knife
  (or 1 teaspoon vanilla extract)

For the wine syrup:
2 cups red wine
¼ cup sugar
5 cloves
1 cinnamon stick
3 ribbons of lemon peel,
  3–4 inches long

Pour the milk and cream into a medium saucepan, and sprinkle with the gelatin. Set aside for 10 minutes to plump the gelatin. While it sits, prepare an ice bath for the cream mixture to cool in later on. Set aside six to eight glasses or ramekins on a baking sheet.

After 10 minutes have passed, warm the milk mixture to 135 degrees F over medium heat, about 3 or 4 minutes. As soon as the mixture is at 135 degrees, take the pot away from the heat and stir in the salt and sugar until they are dissolved. Set the pot in the ice bath, making sure that the water level isn't so high as to risk water spilling into the cream mixture. Stir the cream frequently until it starts to thicken to the consistency of pourable custard (15 to 20 minutes, or 50 to 55 degrees F). Pour equal amounts of the cream into the glasses. Chill in the refrigerator until the *panna cotta* has set but is still slightly wobbly, about 4 hours.

To prepare the wine syrup place the ingredients in a saucepan and bring to a boil. Simmer until the wine has greatly reduced and thickened to a syrup consistency, 10 to 15 minutes. Chill. To serve the *panna cotta*, run a knife gently around the edge of the *panna cotta*, and run hot water around the outside of the glass. Be very careful not to spill water into the *panna cotta*. Turn the glasses over onto plates to release the *panna cottas*, and drizzle them with wine syrup to serve.

Paste di Meliga (Piedmontese Cornmeal Biscuits)

Makes 30 cookies

In the pantries of homes throughout Bra, including Irene's, one is likely to find bags filled with the fresh cornmeal biscuits known as *Paste di Meliga*. The original recipe for these simple biscuits was developed in about 1850, after a bad wheat harvest saw the price of flour skyrocket, forcing local bakers to reduce the amount of wheat they used. Corn was ubiquitous and so its fine grindings, unusable for *polenta*, were substituted in for some of the flour. The biscuits were historically made in home kitchens, and their quality does not hold up to industrial production. In order to preserve their artisanal-style production, Slow Food granted the *Paste di Meliga* Presidia status, ensuring that the region's beloved biscuit has a market in which to thrive.

10 tablespoons (1¼ sticks) unsalted butter, softened	⅛ teaspoon salt
½ cup cane sugar	2 large egg yolks
¾ teaspoon vanilla extract	½ teaspoon baking powder
1 teaspoon finely grated or minced lemon rind	1 cup flour
	⅔ cup cornmeal
	1 tablespoon sugar for sprinkling

Preheat the oven to 350 degrees F. Line two baking sheets with parchment paper.

In a large bowl, combine the butter, sugar, vanilla, lemon rind, and salt. Using an electric mixer, cream these ingredients together until fluffy, 5 to 10 minutes. (You can also cream together the ingredients by hand, although it will take longer.) Add the egg yolks, mixing thoroughly to combine.

Using a wooden spoon, stir in the flour and cornmeal. Continue stirring until all of the ingredients are incorporated.

The traditional way to form the biscuits is to pipe the dough through a star-shaped pastry bag into a double S shape. However, I also find them very appealing as chubby little coins. To do this, take a teaspoonful of dough at a time and roll it between your hands to form a small ball. Place the balls on the baking sheets. Press down on the balls of dough, using your index and middle fingers to slightly flatten them.

Sprinkle with a little sugar and bake for 15 to 20 minutes, until the bottom of the biscuits have turned a light nutty brown.

Mary

Fare le cose insieme è più facile e molto più divertente.

Together things are easier and much more fun.

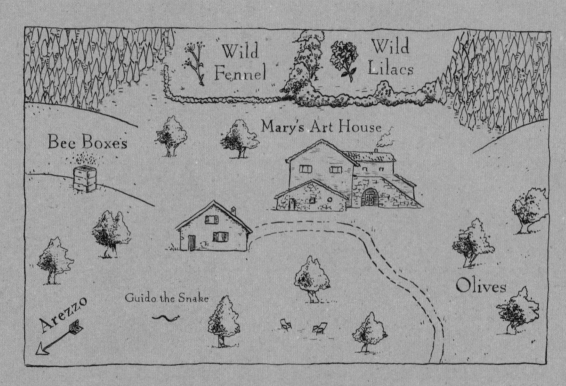

Wild Fennel

Wild Lilacs

Bee Boxes

Mary's Art House

Arezzo

Guido the Snake

Olives

Arezzo, Toscana

Irene had spoken often and fondly about her dear friend Mary, a well-to-do artist and landowner who lived in Tuscany. She felt that Mary could provide me with a new and unique approach to the kitchen and suggested that I go stay and cook with her. It so happened that Carlo Fanti knew Mary as well, and was close friends with her daughter, Marta. He offered to drive me down to their vineyard for a visit one weekend.

I naively packed us a thermos of green tea, some leafy clementines, and a sack of fresh walnuts for the drive. Carlo thought my choice in snacks was insane, and shook his head in total befuddlement. Evidently when Italians take a long road trip, fresh fruit, nuts, and herbal tea are not the foods of choice. If one were to get hungry or sleepy, a more appropriate snack would be a slice of pizza and an *espresso* from one of the ubiquitous Autogrills along the highway. And that is exactly what Carlo ate, while I happily cracked my fresh walnuts all over his shiny, clean car.

We arrived after midnight and the stunningly beautiful Marta was still going strong, laughing with a group of handsome young men at her smoky kitchen table. It foretold the weekend perfectly. Our time with Marta was filled with the pleasures of wealthy Italian youth: physical beauty, dancing, cigarettes, lots of delicious wine, late meals, and extravagant sleep-ins. It was a really good time, even if that decadent style of partying has never come naturally to me. Marta invited me back to stay for a while on my own, which I did the following month, and it was then that I got to know Mary.

Everyone who met Mary fell in love with her. She was softly mesmerizing and utterly compelling; she was intelligent, funny, artistic, authentic, and warm in just the right ways. When I told people in Bra that I was filming her, their eyes would instantly start to twinkle. Even the broody Carlo clucked in admiration and smiled brightly at the mention of her name. Mary was absolutely

"Mary was absolutely everything that I hoped to be as an older woman, and I too fell into complete quiet adoration of her upon our meeting."

everything that I hoped to be as an older woman, and I too fell into complete quiet adoration of her upon our meeting.

It was early spring in Tuscany, and all was bright green and sloshy. Lacy white blossoms peeked out from the bare fingers of winter's trees, while cold-stunted bees buzzed gently in the sun's warmth, preparing to greet their floral friends. Tuscany was fresh at this time of year, sparkling from spring's rain, and filled with pastoral promise.

Marta took me to meet Mary on one of these shiny, wet days. Mary was making soup for lunch, and we were to decide which of the Tuscan dishes she would cook in the upcoming weeks. I don't remember much about the family house, save for it being well decorated with exquisite restored furniture and Mary's paintings of wild hares and black cabbage. As Mary greeted us at the door I was struck by the large and frizzy, slate-gray halo of hair that framed her wide, open face. She had a chic beauty mark above the right side of her softly painted lips and wore a subtle shade of lavender eye shadow. She was the epitome of rustic elegance, well groomed but subtly so.

Mary had made a *minestrone* chock-full of beans, *cavolo nero* (black kale), smoky *pancetta*, and the richness that a few Parmesan rinds had provided. There were beautiful wooden boards replete with *schiacciata* (a flat Tuscan grape bread), hunks of briefly aged pecorino, and fuzzy fava bean pods. The three of us spooned up the warm soup, taking breaks to pop the fresh favas out from their velvety green pods. We ate the favas raw, with rough slices of cheese, after our soup. Similar to Irene's food, Mary's lunch satisfied every hungry part of me, without overstuffing. Irene was right: Mary was the perfect fit for the next stage of my journey, and I could not wait to cook by her side.

Mary had a separate warm-weather cottage that she used as her art studio. This idyllic retreat was just a short drive from her house and had been in the family of her husband, Francesco, for generations. Mary and her sisters had renovated the old stone building, filling the rooms with the worn and slightly broken belongings of their grandparents, all of which held fond memories. The result was a wonky and cheerfully sophisticated house, filled with spring blossoms and lots of laughter. Everything there was inconvenient and amusing to Mary; she even got a kick out of

A Tuscan view taken during my drive down to Mary from the Piedmont.

having to carry in her own drinking water. It was her bastion of bohemian beauty. It was also the ideal setting for Mary's female friends to gather and cook together.

Just as I had, Mary taught herself to cook, alone. Unlike most Italian women, her mother didn't like to do it, and it was hard for me to decipher who in Mary's family was responsible for putting the food on the table during her childhood. When she was twelve years old, Mary just went into the kitchen and began to play with the pots and pasta. Her mother was thrilled, and Mary continued to eagerly experiment with Tuscany's simple ingredients.

The first thing she showed me how to make was *Pappa al Pomodoro*, Tuscany's classic tomato and bread soup, traditionally prepared for young children and the toothless elders. Although referred to as a soup, the *pappa* was, in reality, a sweet tomato mush. Slices of dry, unsalted Tuscan bread were soaked in water to rehydrate, then squeezed of their excess liquid and sautéed with garlic and olive oil. Pressed tomatoes were added, and the whole thing cooked quietly until the bread had disintegrated into a puree. The *pappa* was so beloved that its name became used throughout Italy to refer generally to a child's comforting afternoon snack.

According to Mary, salt had played an intricate and complicated role in the development of Italy's food traditions. Historically, it was too expensive in the central parts of the country for people to buy frequently, and yet it was also vital in the preservation of food. Tuscan bakers maneuvered around its high price by creating the region's most typical bread without salt. Mary used this bread in her *Pappa al Pomodoro*. Tuscan butchers, on the other hand, chose to indulge in copious amounts of salt for the curing of their pigs, the two most famous examples of this being the dry-aged *prosciutto* (from the leg) and *pancetta* (from the belly). Mary told me all of this as she cut strips of pancetta to stuff into her Fennel Roasted Rabbit.

Just as Mary was beginning to fill the rabbit's cavity, Giuliana arrived. Giuliana, whom Mary referred to as the *vecchia cuoca*—old cook—took off her coat and immediately stood next to Mary, quietly protesting. The veteran home cook evidently thought that one must toss the pancetta and unpeeled garlic cloves in salt and pepper before tucking them into the rabbit's thighs and cavity. She claimed that it seasoned the meat more thoroughly that way. Mary shrugged, proclaiming that she herself was a soft cook, a lazy cook, and that Giuliana knew best. This began a string of laughter between the two old friends, which only got stronger when

Clockwise from top left: **Mary. A view of the family land.**
Mary and one of her friends laughing in her kitchen. The family's agritourism.

it came time to tie up the rabbit for roasting. After a heated and amusing debate as to whether the thighs should be sewn together or left apart, they decided to go with the "gynecological position" and slid the rabbit into the hot fire oven with its legs splayed widely open.

Giuliana's arrival was the first of many that spring morning. Slowly, the house filled with women and their suitcases stuffed with presents for Mary and her house. With the arrival of each new woman, the sound of laughter grew louder, windows flew open, blossoming orchard cuttings miraculously appeared in bedrooms, fresh perfumed soaps in the bathroom, and thick bunches of lanky wild asparagus made their way to the kitchen table. Mary's cottage had the capacity to sleep many, and there were extra mattresses and sleeping pads concealed beneath the few actual beds. With each new arrival, Mary incorporated another woman's opinion and technique into her cooking. A friend with dyed red hair, flamboyant and from Milan, insisted that Mary add more raw rice to that which was already simmering in the white puree of *cannellini* beans. This friend exclaimed "no, no, no, no, no" until Mary handed her the bag of rice, playfully threw her arms in the air, and walked away from the pot.

The creamy bean and rice soup was the source of much conversation over coffee and cigarettes later in the day. Mary's method was new to me; I had never seen a grain or pasta cooked directly in a creamy puree, and the result was one in which the grain became fully infused with the flavors of the soup. It was one-pot cooking, which had definite appeal. The soup was also an easy way to cheaply provide a complete protein. The women at the table agreed that eating a legume and a whole grain together delivered all the essential amino acids the body needed. Some believed that this had to be done at the same meal, while others bickered that the grain and bean needed only to be eaten within a day. Regardless, a *Minestra di Fagioli con Riso* was clearly the perfect, and quintessentially Tuscan, way to eat beans and rice.

After the intense inner focus it had taken to traverse the breadth and depths of my learning with Irene and Slow Food, Mary's approach to the table replenished me with the simple pleasures of female conviviality. The meals with Mary were created not by one, but by many. Similar to their artistic collaborations, these women riffed off one another's simmers and stirs. Although I was the youngest of the group and a relative stranger, I was gathered into the fold of these vibrant women and their culinary dance. Every dish prepared in Mary's cottage was touched by the hands of multiple cooks; the result was the most playful and easeful experience of food I had ever had.

Mary's family vineyards.

MARY : AREZZO, TOSCANA

THREE TUSCAN SOUPS

Pappa al Pomodoro
  (Tomato-Bread Soup)

Minestra di Fagioli con Riso
  (Cannellini Bean and Rice Soup)

Cavolo Nero con Pane
  (Bread and Kale Soup)

TWO *CONTORNI*

Patate Arrosti con Rosmarino
  (Roasted Potatoes with Rosemary and Olive Oil)

Carciofi
  (Caramelized Baby Artichokes with Garlic, Herbs, and Wine)

ONE *SECONDO*

Coniglio in Porchetta
  (Fennel Roasted Rabbit with *Pancetta*)

THREE TUSCAN SOUPS

Pappa al Pomodoro (Tomato-Bread Soup)
Serves 6–8

To begin our first meal at her art cottage, Mary served us each a small ramekin of *Pappa al Pomodoro*. The mushy Tuscan tomato "soup" filled my mouth with one of my favorite tastes: fresh, sweet tomato sauce, with its typical accompaniments of garlic, basil, and olive oil. It was no wonder that for decades Tuscan children have eagerly anticipated the *pappa* upon their return home from school. Mary made hers from freshly pressed and bottled tomato puree, a minimally cooked version of what we think of as tomato puree in America. To fully capture the magic of *Pappa al Pomodoro*, I strongly suggest using only fresh tomatoes.

½ pound dry and crustless plain peasant bread
2 pounds fresh tomatoes or canned plum tomatoes
5 medium-large cloves garlic, thinly slivered
¼ cup olive oil
2 cups water
Salt

For the garnish:
¼ cup torn fresh basil leaves
Extra-virgin olive oil

Cut the bread into chunks, place in a large bowl, and sprinkle some water atop. Set aside for 15 to 20 minutes to rehydrate the bread.

Pass the tomatoes through a food mill or blender to create a smooth puree. Set aside until you're ready to use them.

In a heavy saucepan, sauté the garlic in olive oil for a couple of minutes. When the garlic is fragrant and just about to turn golden, squeeze the bread of its excess water and add it to the pot. Stir to coat the bread in the oil and garlic. Add the pureed tomatoes, water, and a large pinch of salt. Bring to a gentle simmer, cover the pot, and cook for 30 minutes. Be sure to stir the *pappa* roughly every 5 minutes, as it has a tendency to stick to the bottom of the pot. After 30 minutes, taste the *pappa*, checking for salt and adding more if you like. The *pappa* should be a mush; if it is too liquidy, simmer it uncovered for a little longer.

When the *pappa* has become a uniformly textured mush, turn off the heat and add the basil. Stir to combine. Serve in small dishes or bowls, drizzled generously with olive oil.

Minestra di Fagioli con Riso (Cannellini Bean and Rice Soup)
Serves 6–8

It took five women to cook this soup at Mary's house! Mary chopped and sautéed the red onions, Giovanna added dried hot peppers, another friend sieved the beans through Mary's rickety old food mill, and two more women stood by bickering about how much rice should be added. One of the best things about this dish is that it is a classic Italian example of one-pot cooking, making it very easy on whomever is doing the washing up.

4 cups dried cannellini beans
Pinch of baking soda
11 garlic cloves
5 fresh sage leaves
Salt to taste
3 tablespoons olive oil
1½ cups small-diced red onions
¼ teaspoon minced fresh peperoncino

1 tablespoon minced fresh rosemary
2 teaspoons minced fresh sage
5 handfuls brown rice

For the garnish:
Chopped fresh parsley
Best extra-virgin olive oil

Sort the *cannellini* beans for little rocks, removing any that you find. Rinse the beans and cover them with 4 to 5 inches of water. Add a pinch of baking soda and set them aside to soak for 12 to 24 hours.

Drain the beans, put them in a pot with 5 unpeeled cloves of garlic, sage leaves, a large pinch of salt, and 4 inches of water covering them. Simmer for about an hour, until the beans are tender. Remove the garlic and sage leaves; peel the cloves of their skins and add the soft cloves back into the pot of beans. Puree the beans with a blender or food mill. Set aside the bean puree.

Peel and mince the remaining 6 cloves of garlic. In the empty bean-cooking pot, warm the olive oil over medium heat. Add the diced red onions, 6 cloves of minced garlic, *peperoncino*, rosemary, sage, and a pinch of salt. Sauté until the onions have wilted and started to caramelize, 7 to 10 minutes. Add the bean puree and 5 handfuls of rice to the onions. Bring to a light simmer and cook, covered, until the rice is done, about 40 minutes. Be sure to stir the soup often during this part of its cooking; it will tend to stick. If the soup starts to look thick, add more water—the rice absorbs a fair amount of liquid. You want the soup to be a pourable, creamy consistency. Taste for salt, adding more if you desire. Garnish with chopped parsley and a drizzle of olive oil.

Cavolo Nero con Pane (Bread and Kale Soup)
Serves 4–6

I ate this exceptionally simple peasant soup with Marta and Mary for lunch immediately after a long walk in Tuscany's soaking spring rains. The dish feels like a walk through the rain; it is wet, green, and elemental in its flavors. It comprises traditional Tuscan peasant farmer's staples: kale, bread, garlic, water, and olive oil. Like many Tuscan soups, it is a good place to make use of bread that is a day or two old—here it is delicious grilled in a fireplace to impart a smoky aroma. *Cavolo Nero con Pane* does well with the addition of a gooey or slightly stinky cheese, and some crushed black peppercorns.

8 cups water
1 teaspoon salt
Pinch of baking soda
4 cloves peeled garlic, divided
2 bunches dinosaur kale, large stems
* removed and leaves sliced into*
* thin ribbons*
½ loaf plain or sourdough
* country-style bread*

Finest-quality extra-virgin olive oil
Sea salt
½ lemon
4–6 ounces Taleggio or Stracchino
* (or other smelly cheese), cut into*
* ½-ounce slabs*
Freshly ground black pepper

Preheat your oven to 400 degrees F.

Bring the water to a boil. Add the teaspoon of salt, pinch of baking soda, 3 cloves of the garlic, and the kale. Boil the kale for 30 minutes, or until extremely tender.

While the kale is cooking, cut the bread into thick slices; lightly rub each slice with olive oil and sprinkle with a pinch of sea salt. Toast in the oven for about 10 minutes, until golden. (If you have access to a grill or ridged grill pan, toast the bread on this instead.) Cut each piece in half on the bias and rub each side with the remaining raw clove of garlic.

Squeeze the lemon half into the pot of kale. Taste both the kale and the broth, adding salt if necessary. Place one piece of bread in each soup bowl, lay on a slab of cheese, pile some kale on top, and then layer on another piece of the cheese. To finish, pour a ladle of cooking liquid over each of the slices of bread, sprinkle with black pepper, and drizzle generously with olive oil. The bread will soak up the liquid and become soft, and is best eaten with a spoon.

Two Contorni

Patate Arrosti con Rosmarino (Roasted Potatoes with Rosemary and Olive Oil)
Serves 6

Under Mary's artistic hand, everything turned to beauty and grace. Similar to Mary herself, these potatoes epitomized a refined rustic elegance. Mary tossed them with a hearty amount of her land's golden-green olive oil, sprinkled them with shiny chunks of coarse sea salt, and then strewed bundles of fresh rosemary and purple flowers atop before sliding them into the oven. There are countless dishes that these potatoes pair well with in addition to her own meat dishes; *Coniglio in Bianco* or braised goat shoulder, would both be good choices.

> *3 pounds small smooth-skinned yellow potatoes*
>   *(i.e., German Butterballs or New Potatoes)*
> *6 tablespoons olive oil*
> *1 teaspoon salt*
> *1½ teaspoons chopped fresh rosemary*
> *4–5 sprigs fresh rosemary*

Preheat your oven to 400 degrees F.

Wash the potatoes and dry them well—very, very well! Cut them lengthwise into halves, and then quarters. If the potatoes are on the larger side, you can cut them into sixths. Place the pieces in a roasting dish large enough to hold them all in one or two layers. Toss them with the olive oil, salt, chopped rosemary, and whole sprigs of rosemary.

Roast the potatoes in your hot oven, for about an hour, turning them every 15 to 20 minutes. Towards the end of the roasting you will need to turn them more frequently to prevent them from over-browning on one side. They are done when they are dark golden brown crispy on the outside, and tender to the bite on the inside.

Carciofi (Baby Artichokes with Garlic, Herbs, and Wine)
Serves 4–6 as a side dish

This is truly an exceptional dish: slowly braised and caramelized baby artichokes, rich with undertones of bright white wine and fresh herbs. It is easiest to make this dish with tiny baby artichokes, young enough that their hairy crowns have yet to form. You can also make it with slightly older baby artichokes; you'll just need to spend a bit more time trimming the vegetables before cooking them.

½ lemon
2 pounds baby artichokes, preferably with unformed crowns
3 tablespoons olive oil
4 cloves garlic, very finely slivered
½ teaspoon salt
1 tablespoon fresh thyme leaves
1 tablespoon fresh marjoram or oregano leaves
¾ cup dry white wine

Squeeze the lemon into a medium-size bowl filled halfway with water. Prepare the artichokes by removing a few rounds of outer leaves, until you reach the leaves that have a substantial amount of yellow on their bottom halves. Cut crosswise across the top of the artichokes to remove the top pointy green part, and also across the bottom to remove the browned bottom tips. Slice the artichokes lengthwise into segments ½ inch thick, scraping off the hairy crowns if they have started to form. Place the slices in the bowl with the lemon water, to prevent them from browning.

In a wide-bottomed pot, heat the olive oil and garlic over a medium flame until they start to bubble lightly, about 4 minutes. Strain the artichokes, and add them to the pot along with the salt and fresh thyme and oregano leaves. Cook over medium heat, covered with a lid, until the artichokes give off their moisture, then reabsorb it and start to stick slightly to the bottom of the pan—25 to 30 minutes. Now add 2 tablespoons of the wine to the pot, gently scraping the bottom to unstick and turn the artichokes. Cover the pot with the lid and cook until the artichokes begin to slightly stick again, about 5 minutes. Add 2 more tablespoons of wine, following the above procedure. Repeat until you have added all of the wine and the artichokes are cooked through and lightly caramelized, 50 to 60 minutes' total cooking time.

One Secondo

Coniglio in Porchetta (Fennel Roasted Rabbit with *Pancetta*)
Serves 3

This was my first rabbit dish, and one of the best introductions to eating rabbit that I can imagine: Its unctuous and herby tastes of wild fennel and pancetta make it hard not to love. Mary gets her rabbits from her elderly farmer friend Settimio, who gladly kills a young and tender one for her whenever she has a craving for this dish. Mary always serves her rabbit with crispy rosemary potatoes, roasting everything in her wood-burning stove. To best achieve the taste of Mary's tender roasted rabbit, I recommend brining the rabbit in a vinegar solution to keep the lean meat moist and juicy during roasting.

For the brine:	For the rabbit:
2½ cups white wine	1 whole skinless, gutted rabbit (2–3 pounds)
2 tablespoons wine vinegar	3 ounces pancetta or bacon, cut ⅓ inch cubes
1 onion, cut in half	8 cloves unpeeled garlic
1 stalk celery, chopped	½ teaspoon salt, divided
1 carrot, chopped	½ teaspoon coarsely ground black pepper, divided
6 whole peppercorns	6 small–medium wild or cultivated fennel fronds, stems removed
1 teaspoon fennel seeds	1 tablespoon olive oil
	3–4 toothpicks

To brine the rabbit, mix the brining ingredients together in a medium-large bowl. Trim the innards from the rabbit. Rinse the rabbit and place it in the bowl. Brine for 4 to 8 hours, preferably 6 hours.

Preheat the oven to 400 degrees F and bring the rabbit to room temperature.

Place the pancetta and unpeeled garlic cloves in a small sauté pan set over low heat. Cook for 10 minutes, to render the fat from the bacon and lightly brown it. Set aside to cool, and toss with ¼ teaspoon of salt and ¼ teaspoon of black pepper.

Pat the rabbit thoroughly dry. Use a small, sharp knife to make a small slit in each of the rabbit's thighs. Once the knife has been inserted, fan the tip out from side to side to make a small,

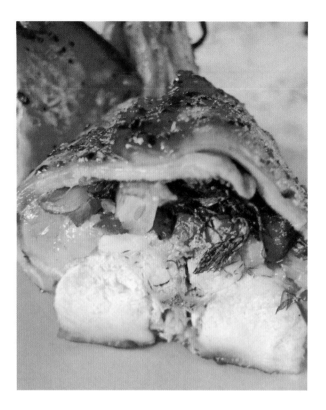

deep pocket within the flesh. Then make small slits on the interior side of the rabbits' forelegs, where the underarm is located.

Stuff the rabbit's thighs and underarms with a garlic clove and some *pancetta*. Add the rest of the garlic cloves and *pancetta*, along with the fennel fronds, to the center cavity of the rabbit. Fold one side of the belly flap tightly over the other and secure closed with the toothpicks. Rub the outside of the rabbit with any fat leftover from rendering the *pancetta*, and the tablespoon of olive oil. Sprinkle the rabbit with the remaining ¼ teaspoon of salt and ¼ teaspoon of black pepper. Tie the small forelegs together with a piece of kitchen twine.

Roast in the oven for 40 to 55 minutes, basting the rabbit occasionally and turning once halfway through cooking. The rabbit is done when it is nicely browned and the thigh is firm to the touch, without give; a thermometer inserted into center of the thigh should read 160 degrees F.

To serve, carve the thighs from the centerline then cut the saddle crosswise into round segments. This is most easily done with a pair of shears, but a large knife will work, as well.

Bruna

*I Conigli: È facile tenerli, ammazzarli,
e sono buonissimi da mangiare.*

Rabbits: They're easy to raise, to kill, and they are delicious to eat.

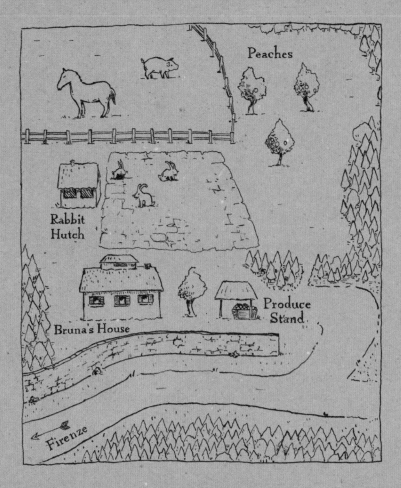

Peaches

Rabbit
Hutch

Bruna's House

Produce
Stand

Firenze

San Casciano in Val di Pesa,
Toscana

There's a parched stillness that overcomes Tuscany in the heat of summer. The intense direct sun hushes the countryside for much of the day. Cicadas keep rhythm with the quiet, and only an occasional voice or passing car punctuates their chorus. At night the mosquitoes come out in droves, buzzing their way annoyingly toward warm ears and bodies.

During my first trip to stay with Marta, I made a stop in Corzano to visit a family farm known for its wine and cheese. A bright-eyed, open-faced young woman greeted me at the family's agritourism, and we became instant friends, sharing wine and conversation later in the afternoon. Like almost all young Italian women, Cristiana had a grandmother who was a very good cook. But the really special thing about Cristiana's grandmother (Bruna) was her extensive knowledge of rabbit keeping, butchery, and cookery. When things came to a lull for me a few months later during the dead of summer, I decided to make a trip back to those magical hills of crumbly earth near Florence to cook with *nonna* Bruna.

Rabbit, rabbit, rabbit. How many ways can you eat rabbit? I entered Bruna's high-ceilinged, stone-floored kitchen and with barely a greeting she began immediately to butcher the first of three skinned and gutted rabbits she'd laid out on the counter. She had a very large knife—the largest I had seen an older woman wield in Italy. She came down on the first rabbit with the strong blows needed to remove the head and backbone. Once each rabbit was headless and halved, she more delicately carved it into smaller portions, fit for frying and braising. It was a striking introduction both to Bruna, and to farmyard animal cookery.

Once the butchery was done, my nerves quieted down and I was able to take in Bruna more fully. She had a cloud of fluffy dyed red hair, a soft round body, and a narrow and tired face. Bruna took me outside and showed me her elevated rabbit hutch; it was quite large, containing five or six rabbits, which were lazing about and nibbling on green herbs and grass. I learned that rabbits were in many ways the perfect traditional farmers' food. They reproduced readily and plentifully, grew to edible size rapidly, and were easily killed. They were versatile in the kitchen, incredibly high in protein (rabbits convert plant matter to protein at an unusually high rate), and made a quick way to feed an impromptu special guest or boost the family's protein intake when it started to dwindle. It was much simpler to raise rabbits for food than, say, cows or sheep.

The way that Bruna prepared her rabbit dishes was quite clever, and reflected the tendency of older Italians to make use of all the little scraps that a whole animal can provide. The juicy parts of the younger, tender rabbits were fried. The tougher older rabbits were braised. And all the rabbit heads, backbones, belly flaps, and little front legs were slowly simmered in a rich tomato wine sauce, then picked over for their softened meat, which was added back into the sauce before serving. That lunch, we prepared fried rabbit to start and rabbit *sugo* with pasta to follow.

We slowly worked through the meal, talking mostly about her family and the land they lived on. Bruna told of growing up in a poverty-induced state of misery. There was sometimes very little in the house: only wheat, oil, and wine. Generally they ate a lot of bread, beans, and soup. Often there wasn't the money for new clothes, and the children grew cold and sickly.

While there was a lot of hardship during Bruna's childhood, her family being farmers provided a certain fail-safe form of security for the children. There were usually eggs from the chickens. They would kill the family pig in the autumn, and that would last the group a long while in small servings of both fresh and cured meat. If the children were sick or grandparents weak, a chicken would be slaughtered for a soup. If a heart was terribly broken or grieving, a rabbit was eaten as a cure for its ache. The children always had peaches from the family trees: fresh in summer, and preserved for them to eat during winter. Bruna's favorite way to eat a peach has always been ripe and warm from the tree, cut in half and filled with cold cream. She beamed with delight when she described eating the sweet flesh from the inside out, with little slurps of loose cream.

Bruna's method for making rabbit sauce was fascinating to me. She browned the rabbit scraps in olive oil, and then topped them with a thick layer of finely ground carrot, celery, onion, and garlic. Her home-canned tomato puree was added, followed by red wine, and then the whole

The church and olive grove near Bruna's home.

thing was simmered for a good hour before the rabbit was handpicked of its tender meat, which was added back into the succulent, rich *sugo*.

At some point I looked over to find Bruna's husband, Ottavio, quietly asleep on a chair in the corner of the room. This long, sweet, skinny man seemed to be playing a napping version of musical chairs; I had seen him with his eyes closed near the rabbits earlier in the morning, and again on a bench outside the kitchen when we went to the cellar to refresh the bottle of olive oil. Quietly he had moved closer and closer to the cool stone kitchen as the day grew hotter.

Once Ottavio was in the kitchen, our conversation became more hushed. I noticed the large oil painting of the Virgin Mary high on the wall, and those depicting various scenes with Christ and the apostles occupying central roles. I told Bruna that I was reading Dante's *Divine Comedy*, and that I was curious about medieval Florence and eating practices during the Middle Ages. Not surprisingly, rabbit came up again. Apparently, as an alternative to eating only fish and vegetables on Fridays and during Lent, people in the Middle Ages could also eat newly born rabbits or rabbit fetuses, which were typically stewed. Evidently the church did not view the very young rabbits as meat, and so permitted their consumption on the days of observance. This struck me as horribly dark, yet somehow perfectly appropriate given the atmosphere Dante's *Inferno* had been evoking for me.

As soon as the tender, egg-battered meat hit Bruna's pan of hot oil, Ottavio popped out of his seat and the grandchildren began to arrive. It was almost one o'clock, Italy's universal lunchtime, and Bruna's family members were eagerly anticipating their favorite rabbit dishes. Despite the whirlwind that took hold of the kitchen as people arrived, that lunch was a quiet one. The children simply sat silently and ate, listened to the cicadas, and enjoyed their grandmother's cooking. The meal ended with us all slurping cool cream out of halved summer peaches.

At the end of my week with Bruna and Cristiana, I left with a fresh perspective on my time in Italy. I thought of Dante's fortune-tellers, with their heads on backward, punished for trying to see into the future. I thought about his vision of hell, and my own struggle to stay in the present moment instead of obsessing over the details of my past and myriad possible futures. My questions and their answers could only be lived out day by day, and all there really was to do was cook, and eat even more. The food and the women once again became my grounding.

Clockwise from top left: **Bruna's horses. An ancient olive tree. A close up of the church near Bruna's home. Bruna at work in her kitchen.**

BRUNA : SAN CASCIANO IN VAL DI PESA, TOSCANA

Coniglio Fritto
  (Fried Rabbit)

Sugo di Coniglio
  (Rabbit Sauce)

Coniglio in Bianco
  (White Wine-Braised Rabbit)

Coniglio Fritto (Fried Rabbit)
Serves 4–6 as an appetizer

For frying, Bruna recommends choosing a small, young rabbit, up to three months in age and preferably under two and a half pounds. Rabbits of this size and age have fine-grained, tender meat, making for a more succulent dish. Before frying, Bruna gives the rabbit pieces a brief soak in milk, followed by a coating in flour and a pass through beaten eggs. While the result is delicious, for a crispier texture I recommend giving the rabbit a roll in bread crumbs just prior to frying. Finally, to ensure a perfectly cooked rabbit, be sure to monitor the temperature of the oil, adjusting the heat so that it hovers just below 350 degrees F. Bruna's crispy fried rabbit is delicious served on its own, or accompanied by *salsa verde* or some mustardy *aioli*.

1 rabbit, at room temperature
¾–1 liter vegetable oil mixed with olive oil
1 cup flour
1 teaspoon salt, plus more to taste
½ cup milk
2 eggs, beaten
2 cups bread crumbs

To portion the rabbit for frying, I recommend cutting it in the following ways:

First, remove the rabbits's innards, reserving for another use. Remove the hind and forelegs, keeping their bones in. For the saddle, separate the rib and loin sections by cutting across the spine; then remove the spine. Cut the loin sections in half. (At this point there should be only tiny bones left in the loin section; remove them.) Roll the belly flap around the loin, and secure it with a toothpick. (You can also remove the flap; it is somewhat tough and chewy, but left on it serves to keep the loin moist.) Remove the spine from the rib cage section, and trim it so that it looks like a tiny rack of lamb. At this point you should have ten pieces of rabbit to fry: two hind legs, two forelegs, two racks, and four loin sections.

Fill a cast-iron or other heavy-bottomed skillet with ½ to ¾ inch of oil; I like to use a combination of vegetable oil with some olive oil mixed in. Place over a medium flame for at least 10 minutes, then reduce the heat to medium-low. If you have a deep-frying or candy thermometer, the temperature should approach but never exceed 350 degrees F.

Combine the flour with the teaspoon of salt. Soak the rabbit briefly in the milk. Thoroughly dredge in the flour, then pass quickly through the beaten egg. Finally, immediately before frying, roll the rabbit in the bread crumbs.

To begin, place one small piece of the battered rabbit in the hot oil, in order to gauge the temperature; it should sizzle vigorously upon hitting the oil. Fry until gold-brown on the bottom side, and then flip to fry the other side to the same color. It should take 4 to 5 minutes to achieve the perfect color on each side, and thus 8 to 10 minutes in total; adjust the temperature if necessary.

Work in batches, frying two or three pieces of rabbit at a time. Remove and drain on a paper towel, adding salt to taste. The rabbit is best eaten immediately, but can be kept warm in a 200-degree oven until all of it has been fried.

The hind legs, being the largest part, may require extra cooking. You can lower the temperature slightly so that they fry for 12 to 14 minutes overall; if the crust begins to brown before the legs are fully cooked, they can be finished in a 350-degree oven without losing too much crispiness.

Sugo di Coniglio (Rabbit Sauce)

Sauce for 4–6 servings

Bruna made use of every little edible scrap that she could lay her hands on. This rabbit *sugo* is just one example: She made it from the parts of the rabbit left over after the meatier cuts had been carved off for a *Coniglio Fritto*, or *Coniglio in Bianco*. The less desirable heads, front legs, belly flaps, and spines were slowly simmered in a mixture of pureed tomatoes, olive oil, wine, and finely ground vegetable and herbs. After a good hour of simmering, the parts were picked of their meat, which was then added back into the sauce. The result is a surprisingly rich sauce, filled with unctuous shreds of meat and herbs. Bruna's *sugo* is best served with a textured pasta, something with nooks and crannies for the sauce to cling upon; fusilli or penne would both be good choices.

2 large carrots, peeled and cut into large pieces
1 stalk celery, de-ribbed and cut into large pieces
1 large red onion
4 cloves garlic, peeled
½ bunch parsley, leaves only
3 tablespoons olive oil
Scraps from 2–3 rabbits: front legs, belly flaps, backbones,
  combination of head, liver, heart, ribs, etc., cut into 2" pieces
15 large branches fresh thyme
Salt and black pepper to taste
1½ cups tomato puree
1 cup hearty red wine
¾ cups meat stock or water
1 pound fusilli or penne
Aged Pecorino and olive oil to garnish

Grind the carrots, celery, onion, garlic, and parsley in a food processor. Alternatively, you can mince the vegetables very, very finely by hand.

Heat the olive oil until shimmering in a wide pot or sauté pan set over medium-high heat. Sear the rabbit parts, turning so that each side is well browned. Cover the rabbit with the ground vegetables and thyme branches, and sprinkle with a generous pinch of salt. Add the tomato puree, wine, and stock or water. Gently scrape the bottom of the pan to release any browned bits created from the searing.

Leave the pot uncovered and bring to a simmer, stirring to combine the ingredients. Simmer for half an hour, stirring occasionally. After half an hour, cover the pot and continue to simmer until the rabbit meat is tender, about an hour more. Stir the sauce every once in a while to prevent it from sticking to the bottom of the pot. Feel free to add more liquid if the sauce is thickening too quickly; likewise, remove the lid to evaporate some of the liquid if you are finding the sauce to be too thin. Overall, it is best to leave the sauce slightly looser than you would imagine; you want to tighten it up around the cooked pasta, rather than having a dry sauce that needs liquid added just before service.

Remove and discard the thyme branches. Remove the rabbit parts, let them cool for a few minutes, and then pick them for their little pieces of meat using your fingers. Discard the bones, finely mince the meat scraps, and add them back to the sauce. Bring the sauce back up to a simmer.

Boil your pasta and toss it with the sauce, heating them together briefly to allow the pasta to absorb the sauce. Taste for salt, adding more if you desire. Bruna served her *Pasta con Sugo di Coniglio* with a generous grating of pecorino and a healthy drizzle of her olive oil; I recommend it this way.

Coniglio in Bianco (White Wine-Braised Rabbit)

Serves 2–3 as a main course

Lemon, olives, and fresh oregano and rosemary characterize this bright dish, inspired by a hot summer day with Bruna and her rabbits. Braising makes excellent use of larger (three and a half pounds or more) or slightly older rabbits; the slow and moist cooking method is the perfect way to tenderize their slightly tougher meat. This braise is also an excellent one to make with hare, as the wild rabbit's gaminess is well matched by the earthy and robust flavors of the other ingredients. This is a dish of clean, elemental flavors, so be sure to use the freshest of ingredients; in particular, use the best-quality olives that you can find. I recommend browning the scraps left over from portioning the rabbit, simmering them with the braise, and removing them before service; they enhance the overall flavor of the dish and replace the need for a meat stock. In keeping with its rustic origins, this braise need only be accompanied by a slice of simple, crusty bread.

1 rabbit
1½–2 tablespoons olive oil, divided
½ teaspoon salt
½ yellow onion, medium dice
7 cloves garlic, unpeeled
1 large carrot, peeled, medium dice
1 stalk celery, peeled, medium dice
2 teaspoons minced fresh rosemary
¼ cup minced fresh oregano
½ teaspoon minced dried hot pepper
¾ cup white wine
1½ cups water
⅓ cup brined dark olives
Zest of ¼ lemon, no pith
Chopped parsley to garnish

To portion the rabbit for this braise, remove the innards then cut the rabbit into the following pieces:

Remove the hind and forelegs, keeping their bones in. For the saddle, separate the rib and loin sections by cutting across the spine; then remove the spine. Cut the loin sections in half, and

remove the belly flaps. (At this point there should be only tiny bones left in the loin section; remove them.) Remove the spine from the rib cage section, and trim it so that it looks like a tiny rack of lamb. At this point you should have ten pieces of rabbit to eat—two hind legs, two forelegs, two racks, and four loin sections—along with some extra scraps that can be added to enrich the braising liquid.

Warm 1½ tablespoons of olive oil in a large pot set over medium-high heat. Sear the rabbit pieces in batches, until dark golden brown; set them aside and sprinkle them with the ½ teaspoon of salt. If you are going to include the leftover butchering scraps in the braise, sear them, too.

Immediately after you have finished searing the rabbit, turn the heat down to medium and sauté the onion, garlic, carrot, celery, rosemary, oregano, and dried hot pepper in the oil remaining in the pan. Sprinkle the vegetables with a little salt, and if they are sticking too strongly to the pot or looking dry, add an extra drizzle of fresh olive oil. Cook, stirring often, until the vegetables have lightly caramelized, about 5 minutes.

Deglaze the pot with the white wine, gently scraping up any browned bits that have caramelized on the bottom of the pot. Add the water, olives, and the lemon zest, and return the rabbit pieces to the pot. Bring the liquid to a gentle boil, then reduce the heat to low to create a lightly bubbling simmer. Cover with a lid set slightly ajar and simmer for 1 hour 15 minutes, until the rabbit meat is tender and pulling away from the bone. Turn the rabbit once during cooking. To serve, remove the butchering scraps from the pot, and taste the braise for salt, adding more if you desire. Serve the rabbit in shallow bowls, with a small ladle of braising sauce poured over the top and a sprinkling of roughly chopped fresh parsley.

Daria

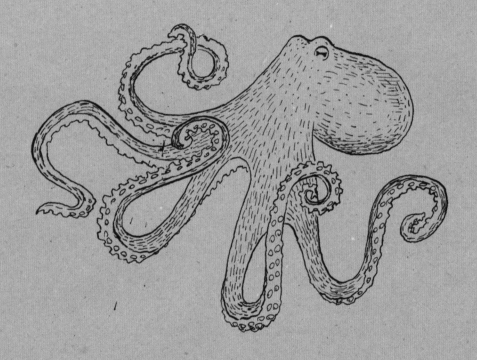

La vita è dura, bisogna ridere.

Life is hard, you have to laugh.

Daria's Basement
Apartment **Biassa**

Cinque Terre Forest

La Speaia

Daria's hut

Calamari

Sardines

Mussels

Octopus

Biassa, Liguria

The little-known region of Lunigiana is nestled between the border of Tuscany and Liguria. I had heard stories of excellent breadmakers living in the valleys' isolated towns, and of women gathering nuts from the area's abundant chestnut and pine trees. I was mesmerized by the descriptions of Lunigiana's forests and its original settlers— drawn to the mountains and valleys because of their magnificent views of the moon—and knew that I wanted to spend some time there. After some research, I found a room to rent on a farm that was near the castled hill town of Fosdinovo and a short stroll through the woods to the tiny hamlets of Gignago and Toffo. Late each afternoon, as the sun softened, I took a long walk to explore these towns and forests, passing the same wild cherry trees and vicious barking dogs as I went. I was slowly getting a lay of the land.

There was a woman named Ori, living with her fiancé in one of the houses on the farm, whom I particularly liked. Ori was fiery yet supple, with olive-oily dark skin and a short temper. About a week after we'd first met, she started to invite me over for lunches and dinners. We got talking, mostly about men and love, and my Italian vocabulary quickly started to expand into the realms of the heart and mind.

Ori knew exactly what I was doing in Italy from the moment we met, yet it took her about two weeks to mention that she even had a mother, and then another week to confess that this elderly mother, Daria, lived nearby and made the best food in Italy. A few days later she asked if I wanted to join her for lunch at Daria's. Ori was a bit territorial, and things generally took time with her. Finally, on July 14, we made our way along the Ligurian coast to Daria. That hot day, and the cooking we did together, marked the beginning of a month filled with pounded *pesto*, shellfish, hand-rolled pastas, and joyous blasphemy.

"During that first lunch
Ori did most of the talking and
Daria did a lot of swearing."

Left: **Daria and her daughter Ori smile and explicate.**
Opposite: **A view of the Italian Riviera from Daria's street.**

The elderly Daria Vittorina Cicci had the foulest mouth I heard in Italy: *porca miseria* (pig misery), *vaffanculo* (fuck off), *porca troia* (pig whore), and *bastardo* (bastard) flowed freely from her lips. More often than not, Daria referred to herself as a *porca brutta*, an ugly pig.

I met Daria in her crumbling basement dwelling in the town of Biassa, a just inland from the rugged coastline of the Italian Riviera. Daria had been born in this shaggy two-room apartment, and was raised between here and a nearby hut overhanging the rocky precipices of the Cinque Terre. During that first lunch Ori did most of the talking and Daria did a lot of swearing. I asked Daria questions, Ori repeated them, and Daria invariably threw up her hands, exclaiming that she had absolutely no idea! Mother and daughter then bickered for a bit, with Ori invariably exclaiming: Of course she knew! She had been doing this for her whole life!

Yes, Daria had been rolling dough for tart crusts, and slowly simmering rice to fill them, for many decades. She had been slapping out silky layers of pasta to be cut into wide noodles; she had cracked egg after egg after egg; she had pried out perfect little nuts from the pine tree's cones, and then she had pounded them patiently with basil leaves until they became pesto, which she used in *lasagne*, or as soup garnish, or simply with a tear of bread as a treat for the little ones. Her wide body had been covered by a housedress and floral apron for close to a century. Our first meal was testament to all this experience: anchovies caught fresh off the coast, her hand-rolled saffron *risotto* rice pie, raviolis made completely from scratch, and lemon liquors to finish us off.

At first Daria hardly talked while she was cooking and seemed to find being watched

a little burdensome. Her hips hurt! Her knees hurt! She was old! She was tired! She had done enough! She wanted peace! Beneath all of this expletive complaining, however, I sensed a quiet pleasure in having the attention of a visitor. This was confirmed when she invited me back the next week, tomorrow, whenever I wanted!

As summer neared its end, our conversations developed and became more personal. Daria talked of her childhood in these coastal mountains, the death of her siblings, the meeting of her husband, and in particular of the Second World War: "During the war we would carry wood on our backs down the steep, rocky cliffs over the shore. We would collect seawater, make a fire, and wait until the water boiled off and only salt remained. Back up the mountain with the salt, and then on to sell it in Turin. It was especially bad during the wintertime, as there were no trains running, and so we had to push our little wooden carts along the trails."

Daria was referring to the historic practice of bringing salt from the Ligurian coast to the salt-hungry provinces in the landlocked north. Salt production and transportation were ancient in Liguria, beginning more than two centuries ago along routes known as the "drailles" that ran from the coast all the way up into the Alps of France and Italy. According to Daria, the practice of salt trading was revived during the extreme poverty of World War II; Italy's transportation lines were crippled, and people still needed and would pay a good price for salt. The historic routes Daria chose bypassed the main roads and railways, and so she avoided the raiding that commonly befell the salt carriers.

Daria's life and food were raw, exposed, and direct; they referenced and reproduced the feeling of sea and rock, steep hills and dark forests. She frequently spoke of tenderizing large octopi by bashing them on the rocks along the coast of the Cinque Terre. When she was a young girl her father would frequently fish for the eight-legged sea creatures, and also the red-fleshed Monterosso anchovies that were abundant along this part of the Riviera and caught by net at night.

Daria was raised in the same town as her late husband. She remembered him leaving their coastal home, when she was a child, to join the Italian army. A year and a half later he returned to Liguria by foot, at which time he set eyes on the newly blossomed Daria. Daria particularly likes to emphasize that he did not recognize her at first sight, and upon realizing who she was immediately sought her hand in marriage.

Clockwise from top left: Foraged porcini mushrooms for our last lunch together. Daria shakes out her *pappardelle* noodles. Daria watches over the family meal. Zucchini plants near Daria's house.

According to Daria, her late husband was good at everything. Of particular annoyance to her, though, was how quickly and easily he found porcini mushrooms when they went hunting for them together. He would enter a part of the forest, and immediately say, "In this place there is a mushroom." Even if they were covered by leaves and invisible to the eye, he could always sense if there were porcini nearby. Daria would look and look and not be able to find them. *"Oh, vaffanculo!"* "Oh, fuck off," she would say to him each time they went into the woods together. Once she even went to the bathroom under a tree where there were almost twenty growing, and still didn't spot the mushrooms.

Our last meal together was the best, and Daria had obviously gone to great lengths to find our ingredients. When I arrived that early-September morning, Daria took me by the hand to the kitchen table and slowly lifted up the cloth covering her woven basket. It was filled with fresh porcini mushrooms. Despite her grumbling and swearing at their dirt and little worms, you could tell she was immensely proud of the bounty she had found. Even her husband would have shaken his head in a little laugh of pride, had he been alive to see this.

Our extravagant final lunch was porcini two ways. For our appetizer, we cut the prettiest ones into thick slabs, lightly floured and deeply fried them. Then for our main course Daria rolled out soft wide *pappardelle* using her hips and the rolling pin; these were dressed with a slowly simmered sauce of chopped fresh porcini, tomatoes, and garlic. As usual, the meal ended with Daria's lemon liquors, some tipsy laughter, and Daria's crass jokes.

"Daria's life and food were raw, exposed, and direct; they referenced and reproduced the feeling of sea and rock, steep hills and dark forests."

Left: The village of Manarola, one of the Cinque Terre towns.
Opposite: A view of Daria washing dishes inside her kitchen.

Daria : Biassa, Liguria

Menu One

Alici Lessate
    (Rosemary Steamed Anchovies)

Lasagne al Pesto
    (*Pesto* Lasagna)

Menu Two

Cozze Ripiene
    (Stuffed Mussels)

Minestrone di Verdura con Pesto
    (Vegetable Minestrone with *Pesto*)

Torta di Riso
    (Saffron-Rice Pie with Spiced Tomato Jam)

Menu Three

Porcini Fritti
    (Fried Fresh Porcini)

Pappardelle con Sugo di Porcini
    (Pappardelle Pasta with Porcini-Tomato Sauce)

Menu One

Alici Lessate (Rosemary Steamed Anchovies)
Serves 6–8 as an appetizer, 4–6 as a main course

The waters off the coast of the Cinque Terre in Liguria are renowned for their schools of glistening anchovies and octopi. Daria was raised above the rocky precipices, often fishing with her father, and always helping to clean the day's catch. By the time I met her Daria was too old to fish, and her joints ached in pain when she attempted the steep climb down to the beloved waters of her childhood. Still, she loved her local seafood, and so I brought her a treat from the sea every time I visited: varieties of dark and shiny mussels, the special anchovies of Monterosso, and baby octopi. Daria liked to simmer her anchovies in a little lemon and rosemary water, though for a bolder flavor, I recommend steaming the anchovies over a bed of fresh rosemary sprigs. The herb infuses the iridescent fish with an exotic woody perfume.

2 pounds fresh anchovies or sardines
A few large handfuls of fresh rosemary branches
Best-quality extra-virgin olive oil
2 lemons
Flaky sea salt

To prepare the anchovies, slit each fish's belly with a small sharp knife. Remove the innards, and flush the insides of the fish under cold running water. While the water is running, gently rub the fish from tail to head to remove the scales.

Rinse the rosemary and place it in the bottom of a wide skillet or pot. Add ½ inch of water to the bottom of the pot, and set it over medium heat. Bring to a boil. Once the pot is sending off a strong roll of steam, place the anchovies on top of the bed of rosemary, cover the pot, and steam until their flesh has just turned creamy, about 3 minutes for anchovies or 5 to 6 minutes for sardines.

The anchovies can be served whole, or de-boned by lifting the spine and small bones out in one swoop with the lifting away of the fish's tail. Either way, these anchovies are best eaten simply, with a drizzle of great olive oil, a squeeze of lemon, and a sprinkling of crunchy or flaky sea salt to taste.

Lasagne al Pesto (*Pesto* Lasagna)
Serves 6-8

Pesto, traditionally a hand-pounded paste of basil, garlic, and pine nuts, is the sauce for which Ligurian cuisine became world-famous. The basil growing along the Ligurian coast, a variety known as Genovese, is believed to be a symbol of love, an association that makes perfect sense given the hours and effort it took to hand-pound enough of it to make *pesto* for the whole family. The beloved emerald-green sauce takes center stage in this lasagna and gives it a wonderful bright and nutty flavor.

Daria does something unusual with her noodles for this recipe: She rolls them out ultrathin and does not parboil them before assembling the lasagna. Instead, the pasta cooks slowly in a thin béchamel mixed with the *pesto*, absorbing their flavors during its time in the oven. The result is a creamy, sturdy lasagna.

For the pasta:
10½ ounces (2 cups and 6 tablespoons)
   type 00 pasta flour
3 large eggs at room temperature

For the béchamel sauce:
½ cup (1 stick) unsalted butter
5 tablespoons flour
4 cups whole milk
⅛ teaspoon ground nutmeg
½ teaspoon salt
⅛ teaspoon freshly ground white pepper
   (optional)

For the *pesto*:
3 cups dry, clean, and very tightly
   packed basil leaves
5 small–medium cloves garlic,
   roughly chopped
¾ cup olive oil
½ cup lightly toasted pine nuts
2 cups (4½ ounces) freshly grated
   Grana di Padana or Parmesan cheese
Zest of 2 lemons
½–¾ teaspoon salt

For final assembly:
2 large balls fresh mozzarella,
   torn into small pieces
2 ounces (1 cup) freshly grated
   Parmesan cheese

To prepare the pasta, mound the flour onto a clean work surface. Make a well in the middle, and crack the eggs into the well. Scramble the eggs together with your fingertips or a fork. Slowly begin to incorporate the flour, starting from the inner edges of the well. Mix in the flour until the dough becomes a shaggy mass.

Once the dough is a rough mass, knead it for about 10 minutes, until it becomes a smooth, pliant ball. Cover with a clean towel or plastic wrap, and set aside to rest for 15 minutes.

Now cut your dough into four pieces. Using a machine to roll out the pasta, take each piece and roll it first on the widest setting. Pass through once on this level, and then fold the dough in thirds, and pass through again. One you have done this four times for each of the four pieces, increase the setting to number 2, and pass each piece of dough through at this level. Lay the dough to rest on the floured towels between rolling.

Repeat this procedure for each piece of dough, at each level, until you get to setting number 6; pass each piece of dough through number 6 twice. Set the sheets of pasta aside covered by a clean cloth until assembly. If you prefer to use a parboiled pasta for a silkier lasagna, now would be the time to boil the sheets, making sure to set them onto clean towels to dry before assembly.

To prepare the béchamel sauce, melt the butter over low heat in a heavy-bottomed pot. As soon as it has all melted, stir in the flour. Stir continuously for 2 to 3 minutes over low heat, and do not allow the mixture to color.

Add the milk very slowly, stirring continuously to prevent lumps from forming. It is critical that you proceed with self-restraint at this point. For the first few additions of milk, add only 2 tablespoons at a time, stirring constantly and quickly to incorporate it before adding in more. After ⅓ cup milk has been added this way, you can drizzle the rest in a slow, consistent stream, stirring all the while to create a silky sauce.

Bring the béchamel to a gentle simmer, and cook for about 20 minutes, until it very lightly coats the back of a spoon and has the consistency of pourable heavy cream. Please stir the béchamel throughout its cooking, or else it

will stick and burn. When the béchamel is done, turn off the heat, and whisk in the nutmeg, salt, and ground pepper. Cover the pot with a lid set slightly ajar, and set aside until you assemble the lasagna.

To prepare the *pesto*, place the basil, garlic, and olive oil in a food processor. Process continuously or in pulses until the basil is pureed, about 15 seconds. Add the pine nuts, grated cheese, lemon zest, and salt. Pulse only for a few more seconds, until the ingredients have combined into a rough paste.

Preheat the oven to 375 degrees F.

To assemble the lasagna, whisk together the béchamel sauce and the *pesto*. Spread a ladle of the *pesto* béchamel on the bottom of a 9 x 13 inch baking dish. Place a layer of pasta on top and layer with another small ladle of *pesto* béchamel, a sprinkling of mozzarella pieces, and a dusting of grated Parmesan. Add another layer of pasta, and then the same toppings. Continue with all the layers in this way, finishing with a layer of *pesto* béchamel and Parmesan.

Bake for 45 minutes to an hour, until the lasagna has puffed up and turned crispy and golden brown.

MENU TWO

Cozze Ripiene (Stuffed Mussels)
Serves 6 as an appetizer

One particularly hot Sunday, Daria and I decided to make a whole lunch based on local mussels and clams. To start the meal, we prepared two spaghetti dishes: one tossed with tiny clams and a white wine and parsley sauce, the other dressed with a bright red tomato sauce into which larger clams had been simmered. My favorite thing that we prepared that day was bread and herb stuffed mussels. For this dish, we steamed mussels in a mixture of white wine and onions for just long enough to open their shells. We then stuffed the dark, shiny shellfish with a mixture of oily bread crumbs, herbs, and cheese. The filled mussels were simmered briefly in a tomato sauce, just enough to warm the filling. If you prefer a crunchy-topped filling, the mussels can be quickly broiled in the oven to brown and crisp the crumbs. I think it was simply too hot that day for Daria to turn on her oven. If you cannot find mussels, feel free to substitute clams in the recipe; the procedure is the same, save for clams needing a longer steam for their shells to open.

1½ pounds mussels
½ pound chard, steamed and
   vigorously squeezed dry
1 cup bread crumbs
1 egg, whisked with a fork
1 clove garlic, very finely minced
½ teaspoon finely minced fresh
   marjoram (or substitute dried)
½ teaspoon finely minced fresh thyme
   (or substitute dried)
¾ cup freshly grated Parmesan
1½ teaspoon salt
¼ teaspoon black pepper
⅓ cup olive oil
1 small white onion, cut crosswise
   into thin rounds

¼ teaspoon hot pepper flakes
1 cup white wine
¾ cup water
1 cup tomato puree

For the garnish:
2 tablespoons roughly chopped parsley
1 lemon, cut into wedges

Soak the mussels in cold water for 20 minutes, to loosen the sand and grit that may be stuck to them. Brush well, under running water, and trim or pull off their stringy beards.

To make the stuffing for the mussels, mince the steamed chard, chopping it as finely as you have the patience for. Mix with breadcrumbs, whisked egg, garlic, marjoram, thyme, Parmesan, half a teaspoon of salt, and pepper. Stir well to combine.

Warm the olive oil in a large terra-cotta saucepan, or other saucepan with a lid. Add the white onion, remaining salt, and hot pepper flakes. Sauté over medium heat until softened and turning golden brown, 5 to 10 minutes. Add the wine and the water, and bring to a simmer. Place the mussels in the sauté pan, cover with a lid, and steam for 2 or 3 minutes, until their shells have just started to open. Turn the heat off, and remove the mussels from the pan. Set the mussels aside to cool for a minute.

Pry the mussels open just enough so that you can fill them with stuffing. Press the stuffing down once it is inside the shells, so that it does not escape during steaming.

While the mussels are cooling, add the tomato puree to the wine-onion mixture, to combine. Return the sauce to a gentle simmer, leaving the pot covered so the sauce doesn't evaporate away. Once all of the mussels have been stuffed, place them upright in the sauce-filled sauté pan. Return to a gentle simmer, cover with the lid, and steam to heat thoroughly through, 5 minutes. If you prefer broiled mussels, you can place the pan, uncovered, under the broiler or in a very hot oven until the bread crumbs brown and crisp, 2 to 5 minutes. Spoon some of the tomato sauce into bowls and top it with a few mussels per bowl. Sprinkle on the parsley, and serve with a wedge of lemon.

Minestrone di Verdura con Pesto (Vegetable Minestrone with *Pesto*)
Serves 6

The week before I left the Lunigiana, Ori and her husband held a large gathering on the farm. While the young people were out dancing and flirting in the orchards, Daria remained in the kitchen, trying to keep up with all the cooking required to feed forty people. She whipped up batches of basil *pesto*, adding it to soups and lasagnas. And she put a huge pot of minestrone on the stove, filled with the vegetables that had ripened in her daughter Ori's garden. This soup improves greatly on the day after cooking. If you choose to wait to serve it on the second day, be sure to add the chard and its stems when you are reheating it, as cooked fresh they add a wonderful spark of color to the soup.

Although Daria made her minestrone with water, I recommend using a light chicken stock if you would like to eat the soup the day you make it. Finally, remember to take out the Parmesan rind and half lemon once the soup has finished cooking.

2 tablespoons olive oil	*A Parmesan rind, if you have one*
5 medium cloves garlic, finely minced	*½ lemon*
1 red onion, thinly slivered	*8 cups water or chicken stock*
1 small bulb fennel, diced small	*1½–2 teaspoons salt*
2 stalks celery, diced small	*1 cup finely sliced chard*
¾ pound potatoes, peeled, diced small	*1 cup finely chopped chard stems*
2 cups cooked chickpeas	*½ cup Daria's Pesto (see pages 133 & 135)*

Warm the olive oil in a large pot set over medium heat. Add the garlic and onion, and sauté until softened and lightly caramelized, about 10 minutes. Add the fennel, celery, potatoes, chickpeas, Parmesan rind, lemon, water, and salt. Stir well to combine, bring to a boil, and simmer together for 30 minutes, or until the potatoes are just cooked through. If you are letting the soup sit for a day, now is the point at which you would stop cooking the soup and let it cool down.

Immediately before serving, bring the soup to a simmer, and add the chard and its stems. Cook for a minute, just long enough so that the chard is lightly cooked but has not lost its vibrant color. Taste for salt, adding more if you desire. Serve garnished with *pesto*, a sprinkling of coarsely ground black pepper, and a grating of Parmesan.

Torta di Riso (Saffron-Rice Pie with Spiced Tomato Jam)
Serves 8–10 as a main course

Daria made this saffron rice pie for our first lunch together. There are two important tricks to making this the perfect aromatic picnic tart: Do not overknead the dough, and be sure to stir the boiling water into the rice after it has cooked and cooled. Heed these directions, and you will end up with a crunchy-crusted, creamy rice pie. The tomato jam complements Daria's pie perfectly; cook the jam first, to allow enough time for it to reduce and thicken. This is a substantial dish, and is great to serve to a large group.

For the tomato jam:
3 pounds medium-size tomatoes
  (or the equivalent in canned tomatoes)
1 teaspoon salt
¼ cup plus 1 teaspoon sugar
1 teaspoon cinnamon
¼ teaspoon hot pepper flakes
Large pinch of clove powder
½ lemon, juiced

For the crust:
1⅓ cups flour, preferably type 00
Large pinch of salt
2 tablespoons olive oil
½ cup water

For the filling:
1½ cups Arborio rice
3 cups water, or 2 cups chicken stock
  plus 1 cup water
1 teaspoon salt
2/3 cup heavy cream
¼ teaspoon packed saffron threads,
  finely crumbled
1 yellow onion, finely diced
2 tablespoons olive oil
3 ounces (¾ cup) finely grated
  Parmesan cheese
2 tablespoons minced fresh marjoram
  (no stems) or 2 teaspoons dried
2 tablespoons minced fresh oregano
  (no stems) or 2 teaspoons dried
1 cup boiling water
5 large eggs

To prepare the tomato jam, core and roughly chop the tomatoes. In a medium-large bowl, toss the tomatoes with the salt and 1 teaspoon of the sugar. Set aside for a couple of hours, for the tomatoes to release their juices. Strain the liquid from the tomatoes, and place it with the remaining ¼ cup of sugar in a large saucepan set over medium heat. Bring to a boil, and reduce the juices to syrup consistency, about 10 minutes. Stir frequently.

Add the chopped tomatoes, cinnamon, hot pepper, and cloves. Gently boil over medium heat for 45 to 60 minutes, stirring every 10 minutes to prevent sticking. The tomatoes are done when they have reached a gooey, jam-like consistency. Turn off the heat, and add the juice of ½ lemon, stirring to combine. Taste for salt and sugar, adding more if you desire. Preheat your oven to 400 degrees F.

To prepare the filling, place the rice, water, and salt in a medium-size pot, and simmer with a lid set slightly ajar for 10 to 12 minutes, until the rice has absorbed the water. Turn off the heat, pour over the cream, cover, and set aside for 15 more minutes. Turn the rice into a large bowl, sprinkle over the saffron, and mix thoroughly to combine.

In a sauté pan set over medium heat, cook the onion in the olive oil with a large pinch of salt. Cook slowly until translucent and melting, 15 to 20 minutes, stirring every few minutes to prevent sticking. Mix the onions into the rice. Stir in the grated Parmesan, minced herbs, and the cup of boiling water. In a separate bowl, whisk together 4 of the eggs and stir them into the rice.

To make the crust, place the flour in a large mixing bowl; create a well in the middle and add the salt, oil, and water to the well. Slowly mix the flour into the wet ingredients (with your clean fingers or a wooden spoon), turning and pressing until the dough forms a shaggy mass. Turn the dough onto a lightly floured clean surface and knead for 5 minutes (adding flour as required to keep it from sticking). Set aside to rest for 10 minutes.

Lightly oil a 9-by-13-inch baking dish.

Roll out the dough with a rolling pin on a lightly floured surface, until you reach a thin and uniform texture. The finished dough should be large enough to line and slightly overlap the baking dish. Roll one end of the dough very loosely around the rolling pin, then lift and unroll it over the baking dish, lifting the edges of the dough to allow it to sink down into the corners.

Pour the filling into the crust, and fold the longer edges of the dough over the top of the filling. Whisk the last egg, and brush it over the top of the rice and dough to create a glaze.

Bake for 1 hour, until the crust is a golden brown and the filling is slightly puffed and turning a yellowy brown color.

Serve with a generous spoonful of the tomato jam alongside or atop each slice of pie.

MENU THREE

Porcini Fritti (Fried Fresh Porcini)
Serves 4–6 as an appetizer

Having never been a successful mushroom hunter, Daria was immensely proud to have found a basketful of fresh porcini for our last lunch together. She sliced the most beautiful ones into slabs to fry. Freshly foraged, wild porcini mushrooms are hard to come by even in Italy these days; feel free to substitute other mushrooms for this dish. Daria fried the porcini in extra-virgin olive oil; I recommend using a mixture of olive and vegetable oil. Including some woody herbs in the fry, such as fresh marjoram or oregano, imparts a delicious aroma and delicate crispiness to the dish.

⅔ *pound fresh porcini or other wild mushrooms*
1 cup semolina flour
¼ *teaspoon fine salt*
3 eggs
¾ *liter (about 3 cups) vegetable oil*
1 cup olive oil
10–15 sprigs fresh marjoram and/or oregano
Crispy sea salt to garnish

Wipe the mushrooms clean with a damp cloth and trim them of any unappealing blemishes. Slice the porcini into ¼- to ½-inch slabs; if the mushrooms are small, leave them whole. In a large bowl, mix the flour and ¼ teaspoon salt. Whisk the eggs together in a medium-size bowl.

Fill a cast-iron or other heavy-bottomed pot with ½ inch oil; you'll need ¾ to 1 liter (about 3 to 4 cups) of oil total. Heat the oil over a medium flame until it hovers just below 350 degrees F. It should be starting to shimmer on its surface.

While the oil is coming up to temperature, pass the mushrooms through the beaten eggs, and then toss them lightly in the flour to gently coat them. Fry in batches until golden brown and lightly crispy on the outside, 1½ to 2 minutes on each side. Strain and store in a warm oven (heated to about 275 degrees F) while you fry the rest of the mushrooms. Finish by frying the herbs; they will take only a few seconds to crisp up. Serve the mushrooms and herbs piping hot, garnished with an extra touch of crispy sea salt.

Pappardelle con Sugo di Porcini (Pappardelle Pasta with Porcini-Tomato Sauce)
Serves 6 as a main course

Daria's fresh porcini mushrooms made their second appearance in this wide-noodled fresh pasta dish. While Daria rolled her pappardelle noodles out by hand with a rolling pin, if you do not have experience with this, I recommend you use a pasta machine. The pasta for this dish is incredibly silky; just be sure to have your eggs at room temperature when you make the dough.

For the pappardelle pasta:
15 ounces type 00 or AP flour,
  plus additional flour for rolling
4 large eggs, at room temperature
1 tablespoon olive oil
1–2 teaspoons water

For the porcini-tomato sauce:
2 pounds large ripe tomatoes
½ cup plus 2 tablespoons olive oil
15 cloves garlic, finely minced
1 pound fresh mushrooms, preferably
  wild mushrooms
1 teaspoon salt
1 tablespoon butter
2 tablespoons finely minced fresh oregano
1 tablespoon minced parsley and
  Parmesan, for garnish

Place the flour in a large mixing bowl, and make a well in the middle of it. Add the eggs, the oil, and the water to the well, and scramble them together with a fork or your fingers to combine. Slowly incorporate the flour, mixing until the dough becomes a shaggy mass. Turn the dough onto a clean surface and knead for 5 to 10 minutes, until it's smooth and springs back after you press in a thumb. Cover with a clean cloth and set aside to rest for 45 to 60 minutes.

Roll out the pasta by rolling pin, or with a hand-cranked pasta machine. If you're using the machine, cut the dough into four pieces, and pass each piece through the widest setting of the machine. Feel free to dust with additional flour if the dough feels damp or sticky when you cut it. Pass it through on this setting three times total, folding the rolled dough into thirds prior to each rolling. Once you have completed this, pass the dough through once on each of the successively smaller holes on the machine, until you reach the second to smallest hole, number 5. Pass the sheets of pasta through the number 5 setting twice. Cut the pasta into long strips, 1¼ inches wide, and store them spread out on a floured surface until you're ready to boil them.

Wash the tomatoes, and remove their hard cores with a paring knife. Roughly chop them into ½- to 1-inch pieces. In a wide-bottomed pot set over medium heat, warm ½ cup of the olive oil. Add the garlic and sauté until it just starts to turn golden brown. Add the tomatoes and a pinch of salt, stirring to combine. Bring the sauce to a gentle boil and cook, uncovered, until the tomatoes have broken down and thickened to sauce consistency. It will take about 45 minutes for the sauce to first liquefy and then evaporate to the right texture.

While the tomatoes are cooking, prepare the mushrooms. Wipe them clean with a damp cloth, and trim them of any worn stems or other parts. Cut them into ¼- to ½-inch slices or pieces.

Warm the remaining 2 tablespoons of olive oil in a large sauté pan set over medium heat. When the oil just starts to shimmer, add the mushrooms, a teaspoon of salt, and the butter. Sauté for 10 minutes to allow the mushrooms to release their juices, and then for the juices to evaporate. When the mushrooms are starting to dry out, add the minced fresh oregano and stir to combine. Sauté for another minute or two, until the mushrooms have become sticky and lightly caramelized. Set aside until the sauce is done.

When the sauce is ready, add the mushrooms and gently stir to combine, cooking together for 3 to 4 minutes. Boil the pasta in salted water until al dente, drain well, and toss it in the pot with the sauce. Taste for salt, adding more if you desire. Serve with a sprinkling of parsley and a generous grating of Parmesan cheese.

Armida

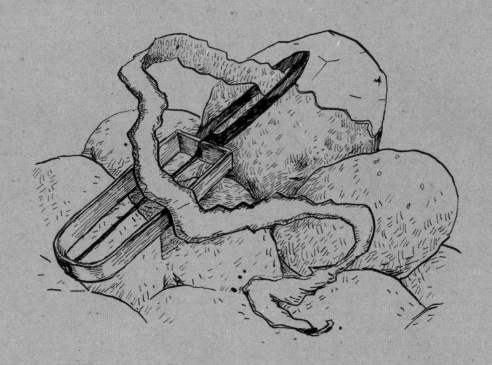

La pace del silenzio.

The peace of silence.

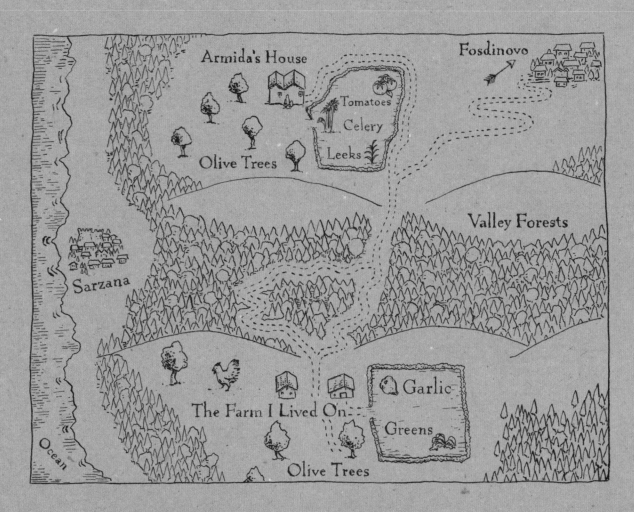

Fosdinovo, Lunigiana

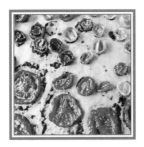

The more time I spent in Lunigiana, the more deeply I fell in love with its rugged hills and mushroom-filled forests. I had come to this wild, isolated valley because I was certain that there would be wonderful *anziane* (female elders) tucked into the hills, making special dishes with the area's abundant earthy ingredients. While Daria had provided the perfect experience of the nearby Ligurian cuisine, after a month in the area I was still searching for an older woman who could teach me local Lunigianan cooking.

The Lunigianans invented many dishes to be baked or roasted in wood-burning ovens, heated with trimmings collected from the surrounding forest; roasted chickpea pancakes, called *farinata*, and *focaccia* are the most famous of these. Whenever I was at a loss for what to do, I would head to L'Antica Forno, an eatery in Sarzana, and settle down for a hot sandwich of *focaccia* filled with a slab of the nutty, olive-oily *farinata*. Anything seemed possible after one of those sandwiches.

One Saturday morning in July, with a belly full of *focaccia*, I went by the local organic food co-op and got to talking with Ivan, a farmer who was in town delivering his lime-green and dark purple figs for sale. Upon hearing of my search for an *anziana*, Ivan told me that he had a neighbor—a very, very old neighbor—who cooked a big meal every Sunday for whoever showed up. He didn't have time to make the introduction, but gave me directions to her house and told me I should go find her and present myself. Her name was Armida.

I gathered my courage and drove the short distance to Armida's house. At the top of the hill, almost at the end of a dirt road, I found an old man walking with his arms filled with wood. I introduced myself, and he said his name was Luciano. I asked if his wife, Armida, was home. *"Sono il figlio!"* ("I'm her son!") Goodness me, I thought, Armida must be a very old *anziana*. Luciano kindly led me down the end of the road and into the house.

Armida was sitting quietly in the kitchen, looking at the floor. She looked to be close to one hundred years old. She had clearly lived many years, many decades, and was now just quietly looking at the floor, waiting. She was listening softly to something almost imperceptible; something still and sweet that I, too, began to hear with her in later weeks. It felt like a rich emptiness, in incredibly slow motion.

Seconds that felt like minutes later, Armida slowly lifted her eyes and gave me a big toothless smile. Neither of us said anything. I just stood there, and we smiled at each other for a few more seconds. I felt incredibly warm and peaceful inside. Luciano then said to Armida that I was an American woman studying *la cucina Italiana*. She motioned for him to pull up a chair for me, and asked if I would like a sip of wine: *"Un po' di vino?"* So I sat down, and we conversed.

Armida spoke in the unique and strong dialect of her birth town, which was a mile away. Luciano had to translate much of what she said into Italian for me, though it didn't really matter—I knew I had found a special friend in Armida. There was a deep, bone knowing that I was in the right place. Smiles and nods were exchanged between us for a good half an hour, and then with great excitement she told me that she was going to make *gnocchi* for lunch the next day. She would love for me to join her for the cooking and eating. The whole thing was too easy.

The next day was typical of those that Armida and I spent together. I took the forty-minute early-morning walk through the woods to her house (it turned out she lived just across a shallow valley from me). She was the only person in the house when I arrived, and was sitting on the same kitchen sofa, blindly peeling potatoes with a small, serrated knife. Round and round, the thin strip of peel grew longer and floppier. The fingers on her left hand were touching, scanning the vegetable, making sure that she hadn't missed any skin. She greeted me and motioned for me to come sit next to her. Together we kept peeling the freshly dug potatoes; we peeled enough potatoes for gnocchi to feed an army. I wondered who would be coming for lunch.

As the morning progressed, the kitchen began to fill with people and food. Family members and random middle-aged women came by to offer Armida a hand. Luciano brought in a dead chicken, then a basket full of eggs, leafy greens, tomatoes, and potatoes. A large rectangular wooden board appeared, covered with old wool blankets. Beneath the blankets were gooey puffs of rising dough that Armida was letting rest for *focaccia*. The word *padrone* was spoken under one woman's breath. The *padrone* was apparently coming that day; everybody seemed to know about

Sunset from my home near Armida in Lunigiana.

it, and wanted to help Armida prepare for it. Once again, I naively asked the forbidden question: What's a *"padrone"*?

Armida's *padrone*, I soon learned, was a shiny, suited lawyer from Milan, with slicked black hair. He was the owner of the land that she and her family had lived on for generations as his sharecroppers. He offered them the tiny, three-roomed house that Armida lived in, and use of his vast property and its products. In return, they had to maintain the orchards and the fields, and give him a part of their bounty. About once a month he would come down from Milan to check on his land, and collect Armida's hot breads, dead chickens, olive oil, and whatever else happened to be ripe from her garden.

For most of her life, Armida actually cooked for an army's worth of people on Sundays. Thirty or forty locals would come for lunch, bringing goods to contribute or exchange with one another. Her family and their friends lined up long tables under the olive trees, lingering for hours over her food. During World War II, army members stationed in the area often came, too. By the time I arrived for my first Sunday lunch with her, however, the typical number of guests had dwindled to ten or fifteen. Armida was now mostly blind, partially deaf, and missing all of her teeth. Perhaps this was why, as with our first *gnocchi*, she sometimes so drastically overestimated the quantity she needed to cook. Or perhaps she was simply still of the spirit that you just never know who is going to show up at your house with a good story and an empty stomach.

Things went well that first Sunday, minus the excess of *gnocchi*. They were light and puffy, and dressed with an incredibly simple, rich sauce made from reduced tomato paste, ground beef, and water. The guests all happily took home the extra, uncooked *gnocchi* for the next day's lunch. And the *padrone* seemed very pleased with both the month's abundance and yet another exceptional meal made by the sweet old Armida. The only person who was not entirely content with the day was Armida herself; her son Sergio had burned the *focaccia*, leaving her with no option but to give the *padrone* a few dark brown slabs. Armida gave out a little cry when she tapped and smelled them, and realized they had burned. For the rest of the lunch she appeared to be on the edge of tears.

The next Sunday morning I arrived to find Armida directing Sergio in the plucking of the morning's freshly killed chicken. He was outside, and she was seated inside, talking to him from the kitchen window. Sergio would dunk the limp chicken into a bucket of scalding-hot water and

Clockwise from top left: **Armida rolls dough for her** *gnocchi*. **A view of Gignago, the tiny hamlet in which Armida was born and raised. A toothless smile from Armida in her kitchen. A view from Gignago towards the ocean.**

pull out the white and black feathers with quick little tugs. Armida would then feel the chicken over and tell him where he needed to pluck more. Sergio, of course, knew exactly how to pluck a chicken. He and his mother had done this chore together on Sundays for decades. It seemed a sweet gesture that he found a way to still include her despite her limited mobility.

I rarely saw Armida outside. As a sharecropper's wife, she had worked the land for most of her life. But now she was too old and sore to move easily. She had the strong aches of arthritis, and her calves and ankles were swollen to three or four times their original size. It was as if all the fluid and physical pain of life in a body had slid down to the bottom of her, where it pooled heavily, bringing her closer and closer to the earth, and to rest. Armida still did most of the cooking, but her sons and their wives were the ones who now worked the land, made the fire in the wood-burning oven, plucked the chickens, and harvested the olives. She just sat in the kitchen, peeling and grating, stirring and turning, and pausing occasionally to take a labored walk down the hall to the bathroom.

In addition to tasting delicious, the ways in which Armida cooked the chicken that Sunday were medicinal and healing for her ailing body. Once it was plucked and gutted, beheaded and befooted (all with her small serrated knife), Armida filled the chicken's cavity with borage, chard, herbs, eggs, and bread. She sewed it closed, and slowly simmered it for a couple of hours. The pale, boiled bird was then carved of its meat, which was served with a drizzle of green olive oil and a sprinkling of salt. The bones were put back into the large pot of broth, a squeeze of lemon was added, and the whole thing simmered for the rest of the afternoon. We ate this mineral-rich bone broth the next day as a soup for lunch. The lemon had acidified the water, draining the chicken bones of their minerals, and the wild borage and chard had given up their green, chlorophyll hue to enrich the broth. We had extracted from the chicken and the greens all that they had to give, and they had become us, reinforcing our bones and tissues.

Armida told me that the broth helped her pain. It soothed the ache consuming her arms and legs. It was one of the only things that she clearly enjoyed eating. Armida told me of how, as a young girl, the family's chickens were used for eggs and rarely killed, as this made more sense for feeding the family. A young and productive chicken was only ever killed for its meat when there was a dire health situation to remedy—a dying child, a mother who could not produce milk, or an old person too sick to work. It was nature's medicine, and her cure.

I knew that the last day that I went to sit and cook with Armida would likely be the end of my knowing her. I was heading south, and had no plan to return to the north of Italy anytime soon. On each afternoon that I had said good-bye to her that summer, I went through a small

The tiny chapel in Gignago.

letting-go. With her, the preciousness of life and time was pronounced, and I felt this acutely during my final walk over for lunch. That day, Armida made the dish I had been longing for all summer: *testaroli*. These were thick, chewy pancakes, made on a long, flat cast-iron griddle called a *testo*. The *testo* was significantly more ancient than Armida; it was thought to have originated in the fourteenth century, with *testaroli* believed by some to be Italy's original pasta. Armida poured the batter onto the hot, oiled *testo*, spilling it all around. She waited to feel the little puffs of steam that rose up from the holes of the ready-to-flip *testaroli*, and then turned them over with a fork and finger. Pancake after pancake, they arrived hot on my plate, ready to be gobbled up with pesto or grated pecorino and olive oil. It was my idea of heaven.

When I finally got up to say good-bye, Armida handed me her ancestor's *testo*. She held me in a long, quiet embrace, and then said to take good care of her *testo*, and to think of her whenever I used it.

ARMIDA : FOSDINOVO, LUNIGIANA

THE CHICKEN

Gallina Ripiena
   (Boiled Chicken Stuffed with Bread, Borage, and Parmesan)

Chicken Bone Broth

Chicken Soup with Poached Eggs and Herbs

Sticky Tomato Fritatta

Roasted Leeks with Eggs and Olives

FLOUR

Testaroli
   (Chewy Mountain Pancakes with Pesto)

Gnocchi con Ragù
   (Potato *Gnocchi* with Tomato-Beef Ragu)

Pasta di Farro
   (Thick Spelt Noodles with Walnut-Parsley Sauce)

La Pignolata
   (Pine Nut Biscuit Cake)

Gallina Ripiena (Boiled Chicken Stuffed with Bread, Borage, and Parmesan)
Serves 4–6

Armida only stuffed and boiled a chicken for Christmas and Ferragosto (August 15, the assumption of the Virgin Mary). We ate the simple chicken together on Ferragosto, and that day Armida told me a story about chickens and her childhood. When she was a young girl, the teacher in her school played favorites, always doting on those children who brought her special gifts. Armida's family, having no money, had nothing extravagant to provide the greedy teacher. And so the creative Armida would pick an apple or a bunch of wild cherries to offer the teacher each day. The teacher looked upon this unfavorably, giving Armida poor grades because of it. Eventually, Armida left the school, and the young girls who regularly brought the teacher chickens excelled in their marks and went on to marry well.

To this day Armida's chickens are her most prized possession; she has many, and the hens all produce dozens of orange-yolked eggs. She said that although she was not able to marry well, at least now she can feed everyone very well. Armida used foraged borage leaves as the greens for her stuffing; if you do not have access to them, spinach, chard, and stinging nettles all make good substitutes.

*1 pound de-stemmed borage and
  chard leaves
3 eggs
2 cups freshly grated Parmesan cheese
1 cup bread crumbs
1 small red onion, finely diced
4 cloves garlic, finely minced*

*⅛ teaspoon fresh nutmeg, or a number
  of gratings
2 tablespoons minced parsley
1 tablespoon minced fresh rosemary
¾ teaspoon salt
1 organic, free-range chicken
Olive oil and crispy sea salt, for garnish*

Bring an extra-large stockpot of lightly salted water to a boil.

Wash the borage and chard. Blanch them in the boiling water for 2 minutes. Strain and set aside to cool for a few minutes, then vigorously squeeze the greens of all their liquid (I find it easiest to do this by using a fine-mesh strainer). Roughly chop the squeezed greens. Keep the pot of water boiling. Whisk the eggs together in a large mixing bowl. Stir in the Parmesan, bread crumbs, diced onion, garlic, nutmeg, herbs, and salt. Mix well to combine. Stuff the cavity of the chicken with this filling. If you have any filling left over, you can form it into little balls, sprinkle them with some additional Parmesan, bread crumbs, and a generous amount of olive oil, and bake them in the oven at 425 degrees F until crispy and browned, about 30 minutes.

Sew up the chicken's cavity with cooking twine, or close tightly using skewers. Transfer the chicken to the pot of boiling water, and bring the water back up to a simmer. Cook the chicken for 1 to 2 hours, depending on what amount of time is convenient for you; this dish offers the cook a lot of flexibility, and is delicious regardless of when you take the chicken out during this time.

To serve, carve the breast into slices and separate the legs and wings. Plate the chicken with a scoopful of the stuffing alongside. Garnish the meat with a drizzle of your finest extra-virgin olive oil and a sprinkling of crispy salt.

Chicken Bone Broth

A slowly simmered bone broth is thick with minerals, vitamins, and naturally occurring gelatin, collagen, and cartilage. Armida loves bone broth because her bones and joints are soothed by it; the collagen and cartilage are traditional remedies for arthritis and bone disorders. Additionally, the naturally occurring gelatin calms and heals the lining of the digestive tract, making it good for people of all ages.

After Armida serves her boiled *Gallina Ripiena*, she adds the head, feet, and carcass of the chicken back to the pot of water and simmers them, covered, for 8 to 24 hours longer, with the addition of ½ lemon. The long simmer, combined with acid from the lemon, pulls the minerals out from the chicken's bones, delivering them into the broth. The bones, and in particular the chicken head and feet, contribute gelatin, collagen, and cartilage. In addition to the half lemon, I often add a chopped carrot and stalk of celery to the simmering broth.

If you prefer to cook the broth in your oven, you can do so by placing the covered pot in an oven heated to 275 degrees F, for 10 to 12 hours. At the end of the broth's simmer, strain it through a fine-mesh strainer and dispose of the vegetables and chicken parts. The broth stores well in the fridge for 5 days, or in the freezer indefinitely. A good bone broth heavily congeals from the presence of gelatin; please do not scrape this or the naturally occurring collagen and fat off from the top of the broth. They are important parts of what makes this broth so healing.

Chicken Soup with Poached Eggs and Herbs
Serves 4–6

After Armida had prepared her bone broth, she cooked with it to create a variety of different dishes. Her favorite way to consume the broth was simply, with only a small handful of tiny pasta simmered into it; she didn't miss her absent teeth in her enjoyment of it. When Armida sent me home with a jarful of broth, a freshly laid egg, and a shoot of green garlic, I discovered my own favorite way to use the broth: I made a simple chicken soup by simmering the garlic, fresh herbs, and Armida's orange-yolked egg right in the mineral-rich broth. Just as Armida described, I found the broth to be deeply restorative, and cooked in this way it seemed the perfect joining of chicken and egg.

6 cups chicken (preferably bone) broth, lightly salted
3 cloves peeled, whole garlic, finely chopped, or 1 shoot green garlic, finely chopped
4–6 eggs
2 tablespoons chopped marjoram or parsley, or a mixture of both
Salt to taste
Freshly ground black pepper

Bring the chicken broth to a boil and add the garlic. Reduce the heat and simmer, covered, for 10 minutes. Season to taste; if you used whole garlic cloves, remove them from the broth at this point. Crack the eggs into ramekins or small bowls, and while the broth is at a low simmer add 1 egg at a time to the pot. I find that stirring the broth gently between adding each egg helps to keep the yolk and white united.

Once all the eggs have been added, place the lid on just slightly ajar; be sure the flame is low, otherwise the broth could boil over, disrupting the eggs. If you prefer runny yolks, cook for 3 minutes total. If you like your egg yolks solid, cook for 5 to 6 minutes total.

To serve, spoon an egg into each bowl and ladle the broth over. Garnish with freshly chopped herbs, salt, and black pepper. There are a number of additions to this dish that are delicious; olive oil, grated cheese, and a scattering of sizzling bread crumbs are just a few examples.

Sticky Tomato *Frittata*
Serves 6–8

Armida had all sorts of tomatoes growing in her garden, and combined them with celery leaves to create earthy-sweet dishes. This *frittata* (a crustless Italian quiche) pays homage to these flavors, and to the prevalence of Pecorino (sheep's-milk cheese) in the hills of Lunigiana. To make the *frittata*, I slowly dry oiled, cut tomatoes; this is lovely to do under a hot summer sun, but is easily accomplished in a low-temperature oven as well. The rich and sticky tomatoes are an integral part of the *frittata*, but also make for a delicious addition to or garnish for many dishes, such as Maddalena's *Spaghetti all'Isolana* or Vincenzo's *Pasta e Ceci*.

For the sticky tomatoes:
1 pound mixed tomatoes
 (cherry and regular tomatoes)
2 tablespoons olive oil
¼ teaspoon salt
Sprinkling of sugar if it's not
 tomato season

For the *frittata*:
3 tablespoons olive oil, divided
1 leek, washed and sliced crosswise
 into thin rounds
¼ cup finely sliced celery
½ teaspoon salt, divided
10 eggs
1 ounce aged Pecorino, finely grated
1 tablespoon roughly chopped celery leaves
1 tablespoon roughly chopped parsley leaves
1 teaspoon finely grated or minced
 lemon zest
¼ teaspoon cracked black pepper
¼ pound soft pecorino or goat cheese,
 broken into small, rough pieces

To prepare the sticky tomatoes, preheat the oven to 325 degrees F. Line a baking sheet with parchment paper.

Slice the cherry tomatoes in half lengthwise, and the larger tomatoes into slices ⅛ to ½ inch thick. Place the tomatoes on the baking sheet and drizzle the olive oil over them, gently rubbing the tomatoes around in the oil to coat them on both sides. Sprinkle with the salt and sugar, and place in the oven. Bake for roughly an hour to an hour and a quarter, until the tomatoes look a little wrinkled and sticky and are starting to brown on the bottoms, but still have a little moisture.

To prepare the *frittata*, preheat the oven to 325 degrees F.

Warm 1 tablespoon of the olive oil in an medium-size, ovenproof sauté pan set over medium heat. When the oil begins to shimmer, add the sliced leek, celery, and ¼ teaspoon of salt. Sauté until softened, 5 to 7 minutes. Set the vegetables aside and wipe or wash the pan clean.

Whisk the eggs together in a large bowl. Stir in the sautéed leeks and celery, the grated hard Pecorino, the celery and parsley leaves, lemon zest, black pepper, and remaining ¼ teaspoon salt. Finally, fold in most of the soft pecorino and the sticky tomatoes, reserving a few for the top of the *frittata*.

Warm the remaining 2 tablespoons of olive oil in the sauté pan, set over medium-high heat. When the oil begins to shimmer, add the egg mixture. Lay the reserved tomatoes and cheese on top of the egg mixture, and place the pan in the oven.

Bake for 30 to 35 minutes, until the top of the *frittata* is almost set, and the middle is still just slightly wiggly to the touch. Set aside for 10 to 15 minutes to finish cooking, then serve cut into wedges. The *frittata* is delicious served warm or cold.

Roasted Leeks with Eggs and Olives

Serves 6 as an appetizer or hors d'oeuvre

This appetizer dish is a tribute to the three foods Armida loved most from her farm: alliums (members of the onion/garlic family), eggs, and olives. In particular, Armida favored alliums, always growing many varieties of them to add to soups and sauces, and to pound into pesto for testaroli. One of my favorite ways to eat leeks is slowly roasted in a cooling wood-burning oven until they become crispy and slightly sweet. Roasting them in a regular oven produces a very similar effect, one that is complemented perfectly by a dip into a soft-boiled egg and a bite of salty olive. These leeks are rich, and make for a somewhat addictive and unusual hors d'oeuvre.

6 medium leeks
2½ tablespoons olive oil
¼ teaspoon salt

3 eggs
¼ cup high-quality olives
Salt and crushed black pepper to sprinkle

Preheat your oven to 400 degrees F. Line a baking sheet with parchment paper.

Trim the bottom tips of the leeks, leaving part of the root intact so that each leek stays together. Cut the leeks in half lengthwise, and wash them under cold running water. Make sure to wash within their folds to remove any dirt. Thoroughly dry the leeks; this will ensure that they crisp during roasting.

Toss the dried leeks with the olive oil and salt, and place them, cut-side up, on the baking sheet. Roast for 35 to 45 minutes, turning once during this time. The leeks are done when they are nicely browned and crunchy.

While the leeks are roasting, bring a small pot of water to a boil. Gently lower in the whole eggs and simmer for 7 to 10 minutes. A 7-minute boil will produce an egg with a runny center, which is good for dipping the leeks into. However, if you prefer a more set yolk, you can boil the eggs for up to 10 minutes to create a hard-boiled, fully set center. At the end of the boil, remove the eggs from the pan and shock them in cold running water for a minute.

Peel the eggs and cut them in half lengthwise, if they were soft-boiled, or in quarters or sixths if they were hard-boiled.

To serve, place the roasted leeks, eggs, and olives on a platter. Finish by sprinkling the eggs with a little salt and black pepper if you desire.

Testaroli (Chewy Mountain Pancakes with *Pesto*)

Serves 8 as an appetizer (makes 20–24 small pancakes)

Armida made me these ancient Lunigianan pancakes for our last meal together. Although they are now typically served hot off the griddle, in times past they were more frequently cut, dried, and then boiled. In this form they are known as *pagnacci*, and are believed by the natives of Lunigiana to be Italy's first *pasta sciutta* (dried pasta), originating in the fourteenth century. Traditionally, *testaroli* were made in a slightly domed cast-iron pan, set over the warm embers in the family hearth. Today they are more frequently cooked on the stovetop.

1¾ cups water
1 cup semolina flour
1 cup all-purpose flour
½ teaspoon salt
Olive oil, to grease the griddle

For the garnish:
½ cup pesto (see Daria's Pesto recipe,
    pages 133 & 135)
-or-
Freshly grated Pecorino
Finely chopped fresh marjoram leaves
Freshly ground black pepper
Olive oil

Place the water in a medium-large bowl. Slowly whisk in the flours and salt, continuing to whisk until no lumps remain. Set aside for 15 minutes to thicken and settle. Check the consistency of the batter and add water if necessary. It should be like thick pancake batter.

Heat a large (preferably cast-iron) skillet over medium-low heat. Lightly grease the pan with olive oil.

Pour scant 2 tablespoons of batter onto the hot skillet to form small pancakes; as soon as the batter hits the pan, use the back of the spoon to spread and widen the batter around. Ideally, you will create pancakes about 3 inches wide. Cook for 3 to 4 minutes on each side, until golden brown. (Interestingly, similar to other pancakes, you will likely find the first *testaroli* to be greatly inferior to those that follow.)

The *testaroli* can be stacked on top of one another and kept warm in a clean cloth until they have all been made; otherwise they can be served hot off the griddle and slightly crispy. Either way, serve the *testaroli* warm with *pesto*, or with shavings of Pecorino, chopped marjoram, freshly ground pepper, and olive oil.

Gnocchi con Ragù (Potato *Gnocchi* with Tomato-Beef Ragu)
Serves 4 as an entrée, 6 as an appetizer

The airy flesh of the ubiquitous russet potato makes it the perfect choice for *gnocchi*. To create light, pillowy *gnocchi*, make sure that your dough is neither too wet nor overworked. Armida uses the fine markings of the back of her cheese grater to mark the *gnocchi*; I recommend using the fine side of a box grater to do this, or forming the *gnocchi* and running them along a wire whisk to mark them. The *gnocchi* are wonderful with Armida's easy, rich ragu. They are also delicious with a simpler dressing of melted butter and grated cheese.

For the ragu:
2 tablespoons olive oil
¾ cup finely diced red onion
2 cloves garlic, finely minced
1 tablespoon chopped parsley
1 bay leaf
8 ounces (1 cup) ground beef
½ teaspoon fresh ground pepper
1 cup tomato paste
½ teaspoon sugar
1 teaspoon salt
7 cups water

For the *gnocchi*:
2–3 russet potatoes (1½ pounds)
1 teaspoon salt, plus more for cooking water
1½ cups flour, plus more for kneading

For the garnish:
½ cup grated Parmesan cheese
1 tablespoon chopped parsley

Begin by making the ragu. Warm the oil until shimmering in a heavy-bottomed pot set over medium-low heat. Add the onion, garlic, parsley, and bay leaf and cook until softened, 5 to 10 minutes. Turn the heat up to medium and add the beef, stirring until it is evenly browned, 5 to 10 minutes more. Add the remaining ragu ingredients, bring the mixture to a boil, then reduce the heat and simmer, uncovered, until the sauce has a medium-thick consistency, about 1½ hours.

While the ragu is cooking, prepare the *gnocchi*. Wash the potatoes and place them in a large pot covered by cold water. Add a generous pinch of salt and bring the potatoes to a boil. Cook until tender, about 20 minutes.

Drain the cooked potatoes in a colander and let them cool enough in order to remove their skins. Peel the potatoes and then let them cool for at least 15 minutes more so that their remaining moisture evaporates in steam; this is important, as drier potatoes make for lighter *gnocchi*.

Pass the potatoes through a potato ricer or mesh strainer into a bowl. Add 1 teaspoon of the salt and all of the flour. With a wooden spoon, mix briefly until the potato and flour begin to combine into large crumbs. Using your hands, press the dough together until it becomes coherent.

Sprinkle a little flour on a wooden surface and knead just until the dough is homogeneous and smooth; it is important to not overwork the dough, as the *gnocchi* can become tough. Cut the dough into four sections and roll out each section into a long cylinder, ½ to ¾ inch thick. With a sharp knife, cut off little *gnocchi* about every ½ to 1 inch, and gently roll them into small balls.

To mark the *gnocchi*, use the fine side of a box grater. Place your dominant hand's thumb on the top edge of the *gnocchi*. Press your thumb across the dough, rolling it down the grater roughly for about an inch. Then roll the dough back up to release your thumb from the dough, and the dough from the grater. In so doing, a concave pillow-shaped *gnocchi* will have formed. Place the gnocchi on a floured baking sheet until you're ready to cook.

Once the ragu is nearly finished, season it to taste and bring a large pot of salted water to a boil. Cook the *gnocchi*, in batches if necessary, for 5 to 8 minutes. They will float to the top when they are done—but do test them, as you might prefer to cook them for a minute longer.

Remove the *gnocchi* with a slotted spoon add them to the ragu pot. Once all of the *gnocchi* have been added to the pot, cook for a minute over medium heat, to tighten the sauce around the gnocchi. If the sauce is looking a little dry, feel free to add a little pasta water to the pot.

Serve on warmed plates, garnished with the Parmesan cheese and parsley.

Pasta di Farro (Wide Spelt Noodles with Walnut-Parsley Sauce)
Serves 4

Farro is an ancient cereal grain, believed to be the ancestor of common wheat. It has been used for centuries in the northern and central parts of Italy, making common appearances in soups and chilled grain salads. The walks I took through the forest to Armida's house provided inspiration for this dish; the flavors of the earthy farro flour combine with the creamy, peppery walnut sauce to capture the sights and smells of those early Ligurian mornings perfectly. Be sure to use the semolina flour called for in this recipe; other flours will create a fragile pasta that tears too easily.

For the pasta:
1 cup (5 ounces) spelt or farro flour
1 cup (5 ounces) fine semolina flour
10 tablespoons plus a touch

For the walnut-parsley sauce:
1 cup cream
2 cloves garlic, minced
½ cup lightly toasted walnuts, divided,
  ¼ cup pounded, ¼ cup chopped
¼ cup roughly chopped parsley
½ teaspoon coarsely ground black pepper
½ teaspoon salt to taste

To make the pasta, mix the flours together in a large bowl. Make a well in the center, and pour the water into the well. Incorporate the flour into the water with your fingertips until the dough turns into a shaggy mass. Knead the dough until it has become even in texture and springs back when you press a thumb into it, about 10 minutes. Don't worry if the dough starts out a little dry; it will become moist as you knead it. Wrap the dough well, so that it doesn't dry out, and let it sit for at least an hour. Roll out in batches, either by machine or with a rolling pin. If you're using a pasta machine, roll the dough out to thickness number 6. Cut into long noodles, roughly 6 to 8 inches long and ½ inch in diameter. Boil the noodles in salted water for a brief minute. Drain and toss with the walnut sauce.

To prepare the sauce, place the cream, garlic, and 2 tablespoons of pounded walnuts in a large sauté pan. Simmer the creamy mixture over medium heat until it has reduced by about half, around 10 minutes, stirring every couple of minutes to make sure it doesn't stick. Add the chopped walnuts, and then the drained spelt noodles, parsley, and black pepper. Toss to combine and taste for salt, adding more if desired.

La Pignolata (Pine Nut Biscuit Cake)
Makes one 9-inch cake

When Armida was young and agile, she loved to climb the nearby coastal pine trees, gathering their cones for nuts. One homesick afternoon, I stopped by her house to sit with her quietly on the kitchen sofa. I told her how I was feeling, and she drew me in close, holding my hand for comfort. After a long period of silence together, she hoisted herself up out of the sofa and began to fumble around in the cupboards for ingredients. She thought that her favorite childhood dessert, a simple caked filled with pine nuts and lemon zest, was all I needed. She was right.

½ cup (1 stick) butter, softened
⅓ cup sugar
2 teaspoons lemon zest
¼ teaspoon finely chopped fresh rosemary
2 egg yolks
Pinch of salt
1¼ cups flour
½ cup plus 2 tablespoons lightly toasted pine nuts
1 egg white, for glazing the cake
1 tablespoon sugar, for cake top

Preheat your oven to 350 degrees F and butter a 9-inch cake pan.

Cream together the soft butter and sugar. Then mix in the lemon zest, chopped rosemary, egg yolks, and pinch of salt. Stir in the flour and ½ cup of the pine nuts. At a certain point, you may need to use your hands to form a coherent dough. Using your knuckles, press the dough into the cake pan to make a rough dough of even thickness. Cover closely with plastic wrap, and let the dough rest for at least half an hour and up to 24 hours.

Just before baking, sprinkle the dough with the remaining 2 tablespoons of pine nuts, brush with the egg white, and sprinkle with the tablespoon of sugar.

Bake the *Pignolata* for 40 to 50 minutes, until the thin cake has turned a light nutty brown and is pulling away from the edges of the pan. Set aside to cool.

To serve, slice into thin wedges.

Usha

Niente importa davvero e la vita è sempre come un sogno.

Nothing really matters and life is always a dream.

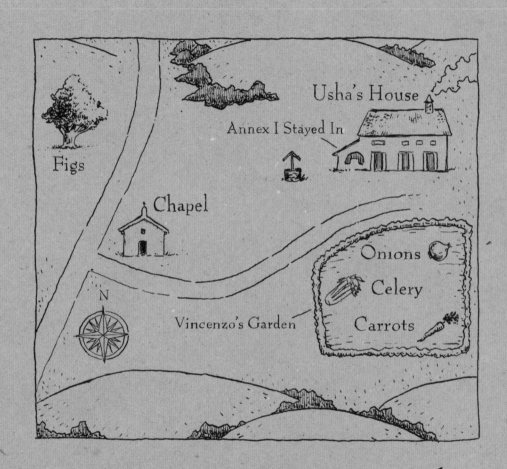

Figs

Usha's House

Annex I Stayed In

Chapel

Onions

Celery

N

Vincenzo's Garden

Carrots

Senigallia, Le Marche

Five years before I went to Italy I had an unexpected experience along the Big Sur coast. I spent an evening "vision questing" to the rattle and drum of a shaman. I was convinced by a California hippie that going on a shamanic journey could show me important things about myself and my future. I was highly skeptical, but also open to all sorts of new things, and decided it was worth joining the group in a "quest." We were each going searching for our "personal medicine," the reason for which we were born.

We assumed our positions, lying on the carpeted floor, eyes blindfolded with bandannas. The shaman instructed us to call to mind a place that we could climb up—a familiar roof, tree, or set of stairs. Once the drumming began, I was to visualize rising up from this place, making sure to remember the exact route I took, so that my spirit could find its way back down. I was certain that I would spend the next half an hour bored and spaced out on the floor. The drum slowly, mysteriously rose in volume—*thump thump thump*—getting louder and louder until it was almost deafening. The rest was magic.

I have no idea how vision questing works, but am absolutely convinced from that experience that something immensely powerful, and way beyond the reaches of my skepticism and imagination, happened. Wild things flashed before my eyes; I went to mysterious places, met still-unfamiliar people, and watched myself learning something very important from an older woman. All this happened on a grungy carpet, in half an hour.

One stormy night five years later, I arrived at Usha's stone house in the hills outside Senigallia and went into utter shock upon meeting the exact woman I had seen in my vision quest. Blustery winds, slanted rain, a dimly lit house. I knocked loudly and the wide wood door creaked open; a beautiful woman with silky straight gray hair stood in the doorway, her garments all white, flowing and glowing. Usha showed me inside and to my room under the roof of the annex. She was ready to retire for the evening, but instructed me to eat some of the simple, brothy soup that her husband Vincenzo had made.

By the time I made it to Usha and Vincenzo's house, I was sick and exhausted. Before arriving in the Marche, I'd had to lie down for a number of hours after each meal, and really would have preferred to spend all day in bed. I had no idea what was going on in my body and why, and was unsure of where to turn. A university friend was closely acquainted with a yoga teacher in Italy, Usha. She recommended that I call Usha, both because her house would be a good place to recuperate, and also because she would know of women I could cook with in the Senigallia area.

When I woke the next morning, the storm had passed, leaving the atmosphere in a hazy shimmer. The soft hills and valleys of the Marche were beautiful: rich muted shades of green and brown, orange and pink. The fields around Usha's house had been plowed into thick earthy clumps, a tractor hummed in the distance, birds clattered in a grove of trees off to side of the house. Vincenzo arrived back from his early-morning walk with a belly and arms filled and overflowing with the ripe Adriatic figs he had plucked sneakily from his neighbor's big old tree. The atmosphere at Usha's house was one of peace, touched with a slight agricultural buzz from the surrounding farmland.

I lived with Usha and Vincenzo for about six weeks; the first couple of them I spent mostly in bed. I was seriously inflamed and puffy throughout my body, devoid of energy, and seized by a series of colds and the flu. My body had just stopped working. Usha, a longtime yoga practitioner, showed me restorative postures, made herb teas from her garden, and took me to town to visit a healer that she knew. Perhaps it was my fatigued adrenal glands, perhaps just exhaustion from too much traveling and relational stress, maybe I needed more iron; no one could figure it out.

During my recuperation, Vincenzo made all of the lunches and dinners. He cooked only vegetarian food, in keeping with Usha's yogic lifestyle; things like a smooth chickpea soups into which he boiled broken-up pieces of pasta, minestrones of every variety, and a spicy smashed

The chapel near Usha's home.

broccoli pasta dish with lots of pine nuts and sun-dried tomatoes. Vincenzo was the principal cook of the house, raised as one of the many children of a hardworking mother. She had taught him everything he knew, especially in the kitchen. Vincenzo loved his food; eating was his passion and his sorrow. A few years before I met Vincenzo, his overfed body had suffered a massive heart attack. The doctor insisted that he undergo triple bypass surgery, and the wise and stubborn Vincenzo got up and walked right out of the hospital. He had read about Dean Ornish's diet, and how it could cure heart problems. Immediately he took himself off all dietary fat and began to take a long daily walk. He lost weight, lowered his cholesterol, and healed his heart. It was either a miracle, or just good common sense. Regardless, this was a house in which healing was possible, for both the body and the mind.

My health took a turn for the better on the morning that Usha made her dense, flaky hazelnut roll for some visiting friends. Whenever he thought of his wife's pastries, Vincenzo would moan and whine "*Povero Vincenzo,*" over and over again. From a desire to keep her husband from temptation, Usha rarely baked her special cakes and tarts. As much as Vincenzo talked about never eating fat, if you put one of his wife's irresistible desserts anywhere near him, he was bound to give in after five or ten minutes of lamenting. That hazelnut roll was a revelation; both in terms of its incredible nuttiness, and because Usha, in one fell swoop, revealed herself as having sugary fingers of magic. Yogini and elder herb-goddess, Usha now took her place as my guru of all things sweet and tender.

After the hazelnut roll morning, my recovery gathered speed. I was already mesmerized by Usha's ability to work healing alchemy; the meditations, breathing exercises, and deep relaxation she showed me had slowly been clearing my groggy, ailing body. And then, when I ate her hazelnut roll, I had a tangible taste of how some of the principles of yoga could be applied to cooking to greatly affect the eater's experience. I knew instantly that I needed to bake with Usha; I was seized by the possibilities that mastering her approach could have on my life in general, and my

"This was a house in which healing was possible, for both the body and the mind."

Clockwise from top left: Usha scooping out a pumpkin on her terrace. The road Usha lived on. Vincenzo cooking in their kitchen. The town of Senigallia.

cooking in particular. The ever-observant Usha saw me sparkle with enthusiasm, and suggested that we host a series of tea parties for her local friends and family.

For the remaining four weeks that I lived at Usha's *Casa della Gioia* (they had named their home "the House of Joy"), she and I came together in the early mornings to bake. We began by sitting quietly together with our tiny cups of *espresso*, waiting for the butter to have its brief chill in the freezer. Slowly, methodically, we worked through her favorite sweet dishes: an airy egg cake topped with gooey nuts, three kinds of apple cake, wafer-thin slivered almond cookies, a plum tart filled with the ephemerally ripe oblong susine, and finally the hazelnut roll. Usha's approach to cooking was one where moderation met indulgence. What could be more simple and satisfying than a moist slice of cake with a cup of garden herb tea?

Usha was tender and methodical with her baking. As dawn rose, she neatly measured out flour, butter, and sugar on her hand-weighted balance scale. Each day the wooden dough board came out, as did a big knife for cutting butter, and small bowlfuls of ingredients—apples, nuts, plums, and on a rare occasion even chocolate. Our baking lessons began with a basic butter crust, one that was used for the bottom of Usha's favorite apple cake, and also for her plum tart. During the first two mornings I sat opposite Usha at the kitchen table and just watched. She thought it more informative for me to observe her technique a couple of times before rushing in to help. Usha bought good, fresh ingredients for her baking, but really she could have used mediocre ones; beneath her hands everything came joyfully to life. The cold butter willfully gave way to the knife in little cubes and shavings, powdery flour puffed and danced about the board, joining with egg in a shiny yellow daze, apples squeezed happily as they were stripped of their outer peel.

On our third baking morning, Usha made our *espresso* and then took my seat across from the dough board. Now it was time for me to make the apple cake, pastry dough and all. She would be there to talk me through any questions I had, but emphasized that really I knew everything already; all I had to do was think of something dear to me while I cooked, something I really loved, and then share that feeling with the apples and butter, the knife and scale. Without a recipe, and with little help from Usha, I managed to make her magical fluffy apple-raisin-rum cake. It came out exceptionally well and, according to Usha, with a unique tasty twist of Jessica.

Over time I have come to believe that if I bring respect, grace, and a moment-to-moment attention to my cooking—or for that matter almost anything in my life—the ingredients can be transformed into an undeniably delicious and enlightening experience. This is obvious and tangible with food (taste and sensation being great mediators), but I have also seen it to be true in both the health of my body and that of my relationships. Usha's primary vehicle for expressing this was yoga and mediation, and mine was cooking; we met over butter and sugar, and I learned about life.

After a month or so of stretching, baking, and breathing with Usha, I was fully revitalized and ready to forge my way down into the raucous south of Italy for the remainder of my trip. Over the course of my life, pain and sickness have tended to point to deeper imbalances, sometimes telling me that I simply need to slow down and rest, and at other times calling me to listen more fully to what is not working in my life. Occasionally, my realizations have initiated loss or change. However, even in the midst of loss, when I orient fully toward health, it always results in greater well-being. Usha taught me this in subtle ways while we were together, and she later summarized it perfectly in a written letter:

I just want to share with you that you can change your energy level from "I am sick" to something else. A little while ago I was really weak, physically as well as mentally, and at my age, ideas of getting trapped into a serious disease are a common ailment. So, I started to change my internal vibration from fear (of disease) into positive affirmations of health and strength. What it needed was a firm conviction, that we are more powerful on the mental level than on the physical level, and that the mind can change the body. I found a strong intention to really be well. Know, that you are The Number One person who knows exactly what you need, and you are also capable to give to yourself exactly what you need. Maybe you have to be honest with yourself and express what you do not want to know? Maybe you have to change something that you do not want to change? A disease might seem like an easy way out, but in reality it is a way that costs too much. I surround you with love and send you a lot of positive energy. Feel it flow into your body, into your soul, into your thoughts . . . and watch where they lead you, when you fill yourself up with beautiful white light. Nothing really matters and life is always a dream. It is not solid, it is an immense empty space, that creates new things incessantly. You are a wonderful young woman and you will find your way!

Lovingly,

Usha

USHA : SENIGALLIA, LE MARCHE

Apple Rum Cake

Plum-Almond Tart

Hazelnut Breakfast Roll

Persimmon-Cinnamon Ice Cream

Vincenzo's *Pasta e Ceci*
      (Creamy Chickpeas with Broken Pasta)

Vincenzo's Broccoli and Pine Nut Pasta

Lasagne di Vincisgrassi
      (Lasagna with Truffles and Prosciutto)

Usha's Apple Cake

Makes one 9-inch cake

This was the first cake that I learned to bake from Usha, and to this day it remains the perfect example of how cooking with feeling and intention can have a tangible effect on the food. I once made this cake absentmindedly and in a rush. The resulting loveless confection still tasted pretty good, but wasn't the ephemeral slice of apple heaven I had known it to be. The act of giving warmth and care to the ingredients really does make a difference, and this cake consistently conveys this perfectly. Usha's apple cake is unusual; at first it seems that you are making a pie. Then, right before baking, you whip up an airy batter and pour it over the filled crust. During the cake's time in the oven, the batter fills out to become a moist crumb, surrounding the apple pieces and covering the top. The resulting boozy apple cake has a rich shortbread bottom and a fluffy, light top.

For the pastry bottom:
8¾ ounces (roughly 1⅓ cups plus
    1 tablespoon) all-purpose flour,
    plus more to dust the pan and dough
½ teaspoon salt
¼ teaspoon baking powder
1 teaspoon finely grated or minced
    lemon zest
10 tablespoons (1¼ sticks) frozen
    unsalted butter
⅓ cup sugar
1 large egg
2 tablespoons milk or cream
½ teaspoon vanilla extract

For the apple filling:
⅓ cup raisins
1 tablespoon rum
1 lemon, juiced
4 apples that cook well
2 tablespoons finely minced almonds

For the cakey topping:
¼ cup sugar
3 tablespoons unsalted butter, melted
2 eggs, separated
1½ teaspoons rum
½ cup all-purpose flour
½ teaspoon baking powder
2 tablespoons milk
2 tablespoons finely ground raw almonds

Preheat the oven to 375 degrees F.

To prepare the pastry dough, grease a 9-inch springform cake pan with butter, and sprinkle it with a little flour to lightly coat the bottom and edges.

Mix together the flour, salt, baking powder, and lemon zest and place them in a mound on a clean surface. Cut the frozen butter first into thin slabs, then long rectangles, and finally into very small cubes, about 5 to 10 millimeters. It is easiest to do this if you coat the butter and knife with some of the flour; this prevents the knife from sticking too much. Once the butter has been cut, place in the freezer for 5 to 10 minutes to re-firm. Spread the chilled butter cubes around the periphery of the flour mound. Make a well in the center of the flour. Add the sugar, egg, milk, and vanilla extract to the well. Scramble these together using a fork, then slowly incorporate the surrounding flour, using the fork to stir it in.

When the mixture becomes too thick for the fork, use a large knife to cut in the rest of the flour and butter. Continue cutting the dough together, remembering to scrape under and turn over the dough during this process. Do this for a couple of minutes, until the dough is in the form of large, crumbly lumps.

Wash and flour your hands. Briefly knead the dough until it is no longer sticking strongly to the board. If the dough is wet, feel free to sprinkle on a little extra flour. Do not overknead. You still want to see the little pieces of butter in the dough; this will produce a flaky crust.

Form the dough into a ball, wrap it in plastic, and place it in the fridge for 15 minutes. After its brief chill, flour your work surface and roll the dough out so that it is about 1½ inches larger than the cake pan. Transfer the dough to the pan and press on it lightly, so that it makes contact with the bottom and sides. Ideally, the border of the dough should come an inch up the sides of the cake pan. If the dough is not high enough, use a floured fork or your finger to gently pull it up to an inch in height. Using the tines of a fork, poke the bottom and sides of the dough a number of times, so that it can breathe while baking. Place the dough in the fridge to rest for 30 minutes, and prepare the cake's apple filling.

To prepare the apple filling, place the raisins in a small bowl and pour the rum over them. Set aside to plump. Place the lemon juice in a bowl. Peel and core the apples, then cut each one into sixteen wedges. Keep the apple slices in the bowl with the lemon juice, tossing occasionally to prevent browning.

Sprinkle the bottom of the pastry dough with the minced almonds. Place the sliced apples in the pastry bottom, making concentric circles, working from the outside of the pastry inward. Fill in any large gaps with leftover pieces of sliced apple. Sprinkle the rum raisins over the top of the apples. Store in the fridge again, until you have made the cakey topping.

To make the cakey topping, stir together the sugar and melted butter. Whisk in the egg yolks and rum. Sift in the flour and baking powder, stirring as you sift. Slowly whisk in the milk, making sure that lumps do not form. Stir in the 2 tablespoons of ground almonds. In a clean bowl, with clean beaters, whip the egg whites until they form stiff peaks. Gently fold the beaten whites into the batter. Pour the batter over the apple filling, making sure that it reaches the edges of the pan.

Bake for 30 to 40 minutes set on a baking sheet, until the top of the cake is golden brown and the edges of the cake are pulling away from the side of the pan.

Plum-Almond Tart
Makes one 9-inch tart

Usha loves to bake with seasonal ingredients. Each autumn, when the *susine* (prune plums) make their dark purple, oblong appearance for a few weeks, Usha makes plum-almond tarts to showcase their flavor and form. While this tart is at its most beautiful when made with *susine*, other plums and stone fruits will also work well here. Make sure that the fruits are ripe—they will melt down beautifully when baked, releasing their juicy syrup.

For the pastry bottom:
8¾ ounces (roughly 1⅓ cups plus 1 tablespoon) all-purpose flour,
  plus more to dust the pan and dough
¼ teaspoon baking powder
½ teaspoon salt
1 teaspoon finely grated or minced lemon zest
10 tablespoons (1¼ sticks) frozen unsalted butter
⅓ cup sugar
1 large egg
2 tablespoons milk or cream
½ teaspoon vanilla extract

For the plum filling:
½ cup fine bread crumbs
½ cup finely ground raw almonds
½ teaspoon finely grated lemon zest
3 tablespoons sugar
1½ teaspoons cinnamon
1¾ pounds ripe plums, preferably prune plums
1½ tablespoons cold unsalted butter
2 tablespoons slivered almonds

Preheat the oven to 375 degrees F.

To prepare the pastry bottom, grease a 9-inch springform cake pan with butter, and sprinkle it with a little flour to lightly coat the bottom and edges.

Mix together the flour, baking powder, salt, and lemon zest and place them in a mound on a clean surface. Cut the frozen butter first into thin slabs, then long rectangles, and finally into

Above left: **The plums cut and in their shell.** Above right: **The plums are sprinkled with sugary ground almonds and doted with butter.**

very small cubes, about 5 to 10 millimeters. It is easiest to do this if you coat the butter and knife with some of the flour; this prevents the knife from sticking too much. Once the butter has been cut, place in the freezer for 5 to 10 minutes to re-firm. Spread the chilled butter cubes around the periphery of the flour mound.

Make a well in the center of the flour. Add the sugar, egg, milk, and vanilla extract to the well. Scramble these together using a fork, then slowly incorporate the surrounding flour, using the fork to stir it in.

When the mixture becomes too thick for the fork, use a large knife to cut in the rest of the flour and butter. Continue cutting the dough together, remembering to scrape under and turn over the dough during this process. Do this for a couple of minutes, until the dough is in the form of large, crumbly lumps.

Wash and flour your hands. Briefly knead the dough until it is no longer sticking strongly to the board. If the dough is wet, sprinkle on a little extra flour. Do not overknead. You still want to see the little pieces of butter in the dough; this will produce a flaky crust.

Form the dough into a ball, wrap it in plastic, and place it in the fridge for 15 minutes. After its brief chill, flour your work surface and roll the dough out so that it is about 1½ inches larger than the cake pan. Transfer the dough to the pan and press on it lightly, so that it makes contact with the bottom and sides. Ideally, the border of the dough should come an inch up the sides of the cake pan. If the dough is not high enough, use a floured fork to gently pull it up to an inch in height. Using the tines of a fork, poke the bottom and sides of the dough a number of times, so that it can breathe while baking. Place the dough in the fridge to rest for 30 minutes, and prepare the plum filling.

In a medium bowl, mix together the bread crumbs, ground almonds, lemon zest, sugar, and cinnamon. Sprinkle half of this (about ½ cup) on the bottom of the pastry crust.

To prepare the plums, cut them in half lengthwise—but leave the back edge of each fruit intact, so that it folds open like a book. Pry out the pits.

Stand the plums upright in the pastry bottom, making concentric circles, working from the outside of the pastry inward until you reach the center. If there are any large gaps, fill them in with any remaining extra plum halves.

Sprinkle the second half of the almond mixture over the top of the plums. Slice the cold butter into thin slivers, and dot them over the top of the tart. Sprinkle with the slivered almonds.

Bake the tart for 40 to 55 minutes, until the pastry is a dark golden brown and is pulling away from the sides of the pan. By this time, the plums should have nestled down into the pastry and released their juices. Serve with lightly whipped cream, or warmed with a scoop of vanilla ice cream.

Usha's Hazelnut Roll

This hazelnut roll changed my life. Upon first bite, it revealed itself to be the nuttiest, flakiest, most comforting baked good I had ever eaten, and it ignited a deep desire for me to get healthy enough to learn to bake from Usha. It marked the beginning of my learning about how love can transform food and cooking, and it remains one of my favorite things to eat. I find a slice of this roll to be quite perfect for breakfast, with tea or coffee midafternoon, or as an after-dinner dessert. The roll is rich and dense, and will easily feed many, making it an ideal treat for a large group.

For the dough:
10½ ounces all-purpose flour
2 teaspoons baking powder
10 tablespoons (1¼ sticks) frozen unsalted butter
½ cup sugar
1 egg
2 tablespoons milk, water, or cream
½ teaspoon vanilla extract

For the hazelnut filling:
2 egg whites
1 egg yolk
6 tablespoons water
¾ cup sugar
4–5 drops bitter almond extract, or
  3 bitter almonds (optional)
2 cups toasted hazelnuts, finely chopped or
  ground into rough pieces

For the glaze:
1 egg yolk
1 teaspoon milk

Preheat the oven to 385 degrees F, and line a baking sheet with parchment paper.

To prepare the pastry dough, mix together the flour and baking powder, and place them in a mound on a clean surface. Cut the frozen butter first into thin slabs, then long rectangles, and finally into very small cubes, about 5 to 10 millimeters. It is easiest to do this if you coat the butter and knife with some of the flour; this prevents the knife from sticking too much. Spread the butter cubes around the periphery of the flour mound.

Make a well in the center of the flour. Add the sugar, egg, milk, and vanilla extract to the well. Scramble these together using a fork, then slowly incorporate the surrounding flour, using the fork to stir it in.

When the mixture becomes too thick for the fork, use a large knife to cut in the rest of the flour and butter. Continue cutting the dough together, remembering to scrape under and turn over the dough during this process. Do this for a couple of minutes, until the dough is in the form of large, crumbly lumps.

Wash and flour your hands. Briefly knead the dough until it is no longer sticking strongly to the board. If the dough is wet, feel free to sprinkle on a little extra flour. Do not overknead. You still want to see the little pieces of butter in the dough; this will produce a flaky crust. Form the dough into a ball, wrap it in plastic, and refrigerate for 15 to 30 minutes.

While the dough chills, make the hazelnut filling: Whisk together the egg whites, yolk, water, sugar, and bitter almond. Stir in the chopped toasted hazelnuts.

After the dough has chilled, sprinkle 1 to 2 tablespoons of flour onto your work surface, to prevent the dough from sticking. Roll the dough out to form a large rectangle, about 2 feet long and 1 foot wide. Remember to scrape underneath the dough, and flip it over a few times; sprinkle a little flour on the surface each time you do this, again to keep the dough from sticking.

Spread the filling evenly over the dough, to about ½ inch from the edges. Roll the long side of the dough over itself, using a knife to scrape under the dough if it is sticking. Roll all of the dough to form a long log. Carefully transfer the log to the baking sheet, forming it into a half circle. Fold each end of the dough over itself, pressing it together to close. Using a knife, cut a zigzag along the top of the roll.

Whisk together the egg yolk and teaspoon of milk; lightly brush this over the top of the roll. Bake for 40 to 45 minutes, until the roll is crispy and dark golden brown on top. Serve warm or cooled to room temperature

Persimmon-Cinnamon Ice Cream

Makes 1 quart of ice cream

This is an incredibly simple, pinky-orange ice cream, rich with the flavors of cinnamon and ripe Hachiya persimmons. The ice cream is inspired by Usha's friend Silvana, who was our most frequent tea party guest. Silvana grew the most delicious persimmons and often brought them to us as an offering from her beloved garden. I like to serve this ice cream with a warm autumnal fruit or nut cake.

1½ pounds fully ripe Hachiya persimmons (to yield 2 cups puree)
1½ cups heavy cream
½ cup milk
½ cup sugar
¾ teaspoon ground cinnamon
¾ teaspoon fresh lemon juice
A tiny pinch of salt

If you are using an electric ice cream machine to churn your ice cream, pre-chill the canister in the freezer for at least 12 hours.

Cut the persimmons in half lengthwise and scoop out all of the gooey flesh. Discard the skins and stems. Puree the flesh in a food processor or blender.

In a large mixing bowl, vigorously whisk together the persimmons with the rest of the ingredients, making sure that the cinnamon is evenly dissolved (it tends to form little clumps unless thoroughly whisked).

Place the mixture in the fridge for at least 3 hours, or in the freezer for about 30 to 60 minutes. You want the temperature of the mixture to drop to at least 40 degrees F, but you do not want the mixture to begin freezing.

Churn the ice cream in the machine until it is the texture of a soft-serve. Place the ice cream in a separate, freezer-proof container (I typically use a glass loaf pan for this), cover closely with plastic wrap (to prevent ice from forming on the top), and freeze for at least 3 hours to firm up.

Vincenzo's *Pasta e Ceci* (Creamy Chickpeas with Broken Pasta)

Serves 4–6 as an appetizer

Vincenzo nursed his heart back to health with this soup, and he did the same for me when I arrived at the *Casa di Gioia* sick and exhausted. Every time I make Vincenzo's *Pasta e Ceci*, I am surprised at how simple and fulfilling the thick soup is. Vincenzo prepared his without any fat, but I find the soup to be superior when prepared with olive oil and garnished with a grating of Parmesan. A touch of minced parsley adds a boost of color and flavor to the final presentation.

1½ cups dried chickpeas
½ teaspoon baking soda
8–10 cups water
1 medium yellow potato, peeled and finely diced
3 bay leaves
8 cloves garlic, divided
2 teaspoons salt
2 tablespoons olive oil
6 tablespoons tiny pasta or well-broken cappellini pasta
Chopped parsley, cracked black pepper, grated Parmesan cheese, and olive oil to garnish

Sort the chickpeas for rocks, rinse them well, and soak them for 12 to 24 hours with the ½ teaspoon baking soda.

Drain the chickpeas, and place them in a large pot with the water, diced potato, bay leaves, and 4 unpeeled cloves of garlic. Put on a lid, slightly ajar, and bring to a strong simmer. Scrape off and remove any bean scum that rises to the surface of the pot. Simmer the chickpeas until they are tender but not mushy, about an hour. Add the salt to the pot.

While the beans are cooking, peel and finely mince the remaining 4 cloves of garlic. In a small sauté pan, cook the garlic in the olive oil until light golden brown. Add the garlic and oil to the simmering beans. You can do this at any stage of the beans' cooking; I tend to sauté and add the garlic about halfway through the cooking time.

Remove the bay leaves and whole, unpeeled garlic cloves from the pot. Discard the bay leaves, and squeeze the garlic from the cloves; return the soft garlic to the pot. Strain ½ to 1 cup

of cooked chickpeas from the water, and set them aside. Puree the rest of the soup with a blender or food mill, then return the whole chickpeas to the pot.

Bring the soup back up to a simmer, and add the pasta. Simmer for the length of time specified on the pasta package, making sure to stir the soup frequently throughout the cooking; the pasta will tend to stick to the bottom of the pot.

Taste for salt, adding more if you like. Serve garnished with chopped parsley, black pepper, grated Parmesan, and a generous drizzle of olive oil.

Vincenzo's Broccoli and Pine Nut Pasta

Serves 4 as a main course

For this pasta, Vincenzo steams broccoli florets until soft, mashes them well with a fork, and sautées them with garlic, sun-dried tomatoes, and pine nuts. The resulting pasta sauce is rich with healthy greens, tasting almost like a pesto. It is a great dish to serve people who are typically resistant to green vegetables; after they taste Vincenzo's creation, you'll likely find them converted into avid broccoli eaters.

2 heads broccoli
4 cloves garlic
1 dried peperoncino, finely minced
3–4 tablespoons olive oil
¼ cup pine nuts
6 oily sun-dried tomatoes, finely chopped
1 pound medium-length pasta, such as fusilli or penne
Salt to taste
Grated Parmesan or hard pecorino cheese to garnish

Cut the florets off the broccoli stems, wash them, and steam them in a small amount of salted water for 15 to 20 minutes, or until very soft. Bring a large pot of salted water to a boil for the pasta.

In large sauté pan set over medium heat, sauté the garlic and peperoncino in the oil, until the garlic turns a pale golden brown. Add the pine nuts, the sun-dried tomatoes, and the soft broccoli. Stir to combine, then mash the broccoli with the back of a wooden spoon until it takes on a homogeneous consistency. Sauté together for a few minutes, then turn off the heat while the pasta cooks.

Cook the pasta until *al dente*, drain, and add it to the sauté pan. Mix thoroughly, heating briefly to combine. Season to taste and serve right away with a generous grating of Parmesan or pecorino cheese.

Lasagne di Vincisgrassi (Lasagna with Truffles and Prosciutto)
Serves 4–6 as a dinner entrée or 8 as a first course

This is a rendition of the Marche region's famed, ancient lasagna. The dish, first documented in the 18th century, is named after an Austrian general, Prince Windischgratz, commander of forces stationed in the Marche. In this quite perfect lasagna, rich prosciutto, earthy wild mushrooms, and spiced béchamel combine to form what would likely be Vincenzo's favorite type of forbidden dish.

While this filling is delicious prepared with wild mushrooms, you can easily substitute button and/or portobello mushrooms. Be sure to include the truffle oil in the recipe; its unique aroma adds an important layer of complexity to the dish.

If you do not have access to type 00 flour, you can substitute all-purpose flour. If you use AP flour, make sure to sprinkle on some semolina flour when rolling out the dough; the semolina prevents the AP flour pasta from sticking and becoming gummy.

For the béchamel:
5 ounces prosciutto, sliced ¹⁄₁₆" thick
3½ tablespoons butter
7 tablespoons flour
4 cups whole milk
½ teaspoon salt
Generous pinch of nutmeg
Dash of ground white pepper

For the filling:
2 tablespoons olive oil
5 cloves garlic, finely minced
1 pound fresh wild mushrooms, or buttons and portobellos, sliced ¼" thick
1 teaspoon salt
1 tablespoon finely minced fresh rosemary
1 teaspoon finely minced fresh sage
2 tablespoons truffle oil
1 tablespoon fresh lemon juice

For the pasta:
10½ ounces (2 cups, 6 tablespoons) type 00 flour (plus more for sprinkling and kneading)
3 large eggs, at room temperature
1 spoonful olive oil, for boiling the pasta

For the assembly:
1 cup freshly grated Parmesan cheese
White pepper
½ teaspoon finely grated lemon zest
1 ounce reserved prosciutto

To make the béchamel sauce, cut the prosciutto into small strips, and divide into 4-ounce and 1-ounce portions. Reserve the 1-ounce portion for the lasagna assembly.

Melt the butter in a heavy-bottomed pot set over low heat. Slowly sift in the flour, whisking continuously and quickly to make sure that no lumps form. Watch this butter-flour roux, and do not allow it to burn. Slowly drizzle in the milk, continuing to whisk, making sure that your whisking dissolves any small clumps. When all of the milk has been incorporated into the roux, add the salt and nutmeg, stirring to combine.

Bring the béchamel to a steady simmer over medium-low heat, whisking it constantly. Over the course of the next 15 to 20 minutes (it usually takes about 17 minutes), the béchamel will thicken to the desired consistency, coating the back of a spoon with an opaque white color. At this point, take the béchamel off the stove and stir in 4 ounces of the sliced prosciutto, and the white pepper. Store the béchamel off the heat, with a sheet of plastic wrap covering the top of the sauce to prevent a skin from forming.

To make the filling, warm the plain olive oil in a large skillet set over medium-low heat. When the oil begins to shimmer, add the minced garlic and stir for a minute without coloring the garlic. Add the sliced fresh mushrooms, and season with the salt. Turn up the heat to medium and sauté for 10 minutes, allowing the juice from the mushrooms to be released and then evaporate. Once the mushrooms turn a light golden brown, add the rosemary, sage, and truffle oil, stirring to combine. Cook for a minute or two more. Turn off the heat, stir in the lemon juice, and set aside until it is time to assemble the lasagna.

To make the pasta, prepare your breadboard, or clean off a surface for kneading the pasta dough. Sprinkle with some additional flour.

Sift the flour into a large bowl. Make a well in the middle, and crack the 3 eggs into the well. Scramble the eggs together with a fork or the tips of your fingers. Slowly begin to incorporate the flour into the egg, continuing to do so until the dough becomes a shaggy mass. Turn the dough onto the clean surface and knead for 10 to 15 minutes. Form into a ball and cover with a clean cloth or plastic wrap. Set aside to rest for at least 10 minutes.

Cut the dough into five pieces. If it is moist in the center, knead in a sprinkling more flour. Pass each piece through the largest hole on a pasta machine. Fold the pieces of dough into thirds, and pass through again. Do this three times on the largest-holed setting (this generally corresponds to number 1 on the machine). Turn the pasta machine to the next setting and pass each piece through once. Continue this process, moving the dough through each of the levels,

until you reach setting number 5 on the machine (the second to smallest hole). Pass each piece of dough through this setting three times.

Bring a large pot of salted water to a boil, and add a spoonful of oil to it. Boil the pasta in batches, for 4 minutes per batch. You want the pasta to lose the hardness in its center, but you do not want to overcook it. Drain it well, and rinse thoroughly in cold water to stop the cooking and remove excess starch. Lay the sheets of pasta on clean cloths to dry for a few minutes before assembling the lasagna.

Preheat the oven to 375 degrees F.

To assemble the lasagna, spread a small ladle (¼ to ½ cup) of béchamel on the bottom of a rectangular lasagna dish. Spread it around the sides. Place a layer of pasta on the bottom of the dish. Spread a ladle (roughly ¼ to ½ cup) of the cream sauce over the pasta, then a few spoonfuls of mushrooms, a generous sprinkling of Parmesan, and a small sprinkling of pepper and lemon zest. Cover this with another layer of pasta, and repeat the procedure, using up all of the mushrooms before you reach the top layer of pasta. On the final layer of pasta, spread only the cream sauce, layer on the extra ounce of prosciutto, and sprinkle with the remaining Parmesan.

Bake for 30 minutes, until bubbling, and then turn up the heat to 400 degrees and cook for 5 to 10 minutes more, until the lasagna is browning and starting to crisp on the sides.

Carluccia

Siamo contadini, ma
abbiamo anche qualcosa di bello.

We are farmers, but we have something really beautiful.

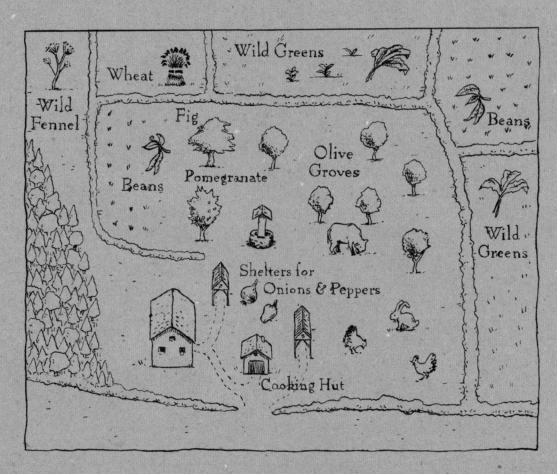

Zambrone, Calabria

The 1,000-kilometer drive to Calabria took about thirteen hours from Usha's, and I felt every minute of it. The farther south I went, the more crumbled and romantic everything became. The autostrada turned sparser and bumpier, the streetlights fewer and farther between. Late in the day when I was tired of eating Campagnian mozzarella and bread, I tried to stop and have a proper meal. All that I could find near the highway were gas stations and one large *mercato* (market), which didn't sell much that resembled food. I continued on, hungry. What an odd and unfamiliar feeling to have in Italy—it occurred to me that I had not been hungry in months.

Once I was off the highway, I drove through my first small Calabrian towns. Shrouded groups of men huddled together under dim street lamps. Laundry hung from the lines outside of windows. There must be a very different mentality here, I thought, where the wives unabashedly hang their underwear within view of the public. Mamma Maria would never have done this. I fell in love with the south of Italy on this drive. It was spicy and gritty. I was excited.

Arriving at *Pirapora*, an agritourism in the town of Zambrone, was like hitting a clean breeze. *Pirapora* had been recommended to me by a friend of Usha's, who gushed about the incredible coastal location. Rose (pronounced Rosie) greeted me and showed me to the simple apartment where I would live for a few weeks. I settled in, then wandered back through the dark to Rose and Franco's home. The children, Sara and Michele, were cozied up on the sofa, dressed for bed and watching a favorite cartoon. Rose and Franco were talking together at the table, enjoying the end of the evening's wine. They offered me a glass of that year's red—fizzy, and chilled from the barrels in the cellar—and some olives that Rose's mother-in-law, Carluccia, had cured.

Rose and I talked about my project, and started to come up with ideas of which local women

"When I finally met Carluccia, the family matriarch,
it was like gliding into an ancient agrarian scene."

I should meet. First things first, though, and a good night's sleep was in order. They sent me off to bed with a large, puffy loaf of the local sourdough bread, some homemade *marmellata*, and a knob of butter.

The next morning, after toast and plenty of coffee (at that point I was traveling around with two stovetop *espresso* makers and a large can of Illy Espresso Caffè Macinato), I stepped outside and was greeted by a vast expanse of blue sea. The islands off the north coast of Sicily were visible in the hazy distance, the sea speckled with white waves. It was windy and beautiful here. I hadn't known what I would wake up to.

My apartment was one of six that Franco and his brother Gianni had built using sustainable construction materials on some land that their parents, Carluccia and Michele, had given them. Carluccia was born, raised, and had spent her life working these twenty acres of land along the Calabrian coast near Tropea. During their twenties, her sons left Calabria to travel the world and work abroad. However, a love of the land, and a longing to continue their family tradition of living off it, eventually drew them back home. They built the thriving agritourism and rented the apartments to vacationers during the summer. Guests beached all day and were fed delicious foods that had been grown by Franco, and cooked by Gianni. Together the brothers were maintaining and modernizing their ancestors' self-sufficient way of life.

When I finally met Carluccia, the family matriarch, it was like gliding into an ancient agrarian scene. I had gone to help with the olive harvest on her part of the family land. Carluccia was bent over under an olive tree, picking through the shiny purple-black olives that had fallen to the nets on the ground, looking for beautiful, unblemished specimens. She appeared soft and supple in parts, and tough in others. She moved with agility and immense self-assurance. Her hair was covered by an elegant aquamarine headscarf, which matched almost perfectly with her nubby gold-buttoned cardigan. Her extra-large, gold-rimmed sunglasses stood out, as did the mismatched nylons that she had rolled to just below the knee. At the bottom of all this, her feet were barely covered by a pair of ragged navy plimsolls.

A view from my apartment on my first morning at *Pirapora*.

CARLUCCIA **206**

There was no introduction; Carluccia just started talking to me about her olives. It was as if we were continuing a conversation that we'd begun sometime before. I was ready to learn more about olives, and she was already teaching me. As I had first approached her she'd begun saying, "When the bucket is full of olives, I cover them with water so they don't get hot and spoil. Later on, I'll wash them well and cover them in salt, with garlic, red pepper, wild fennel, oregano, and a little lemon. I let them sit like this for two or three days. They shrink a little under the salt and herbs. Then, after two or three days, I cover them completely with fresh water. I leave them to age."

As soon as Carluccia had finished telling me about the curing process, she launched right into her favorite ways to eat the black olives. They were delicious with a glass of young wine before dinner, as part of slowly braised meat dishes, or in pasta sauces. Her favorite sauce was made from black olives, capers, oregano, and fresh tomatoes. She said it was perfect with spaghetti, for lunch.

Franco and his brother Gianni were up in the trees, banging away at the olive branches with long sticks of bamboo. The trees were shaking vigorously, and olives were dropping all around us. But for me there was only Carluccia, in her striking outfit, calmly talking away about her olives and their oil. I was so mesmerized I hardly noticed the frequent thumps of olives hitting my head.

That first day Carluccia and I floated between gathering olives for curing, and preparing lunch for everyone else. Carluccia had some things already set aside for the meal, so all we really had to do was make a batter for fried squash flower blossoms, warm up a big pot of mixed beans, and fill a glass bottle with the olive oil they had on tap. As we folded the tight squash buds into a thick batter of semolina flour, water, and eggs, Carluccia and I talked about Calabrian food traditions, past and present. "The young people of today don't know good taste," Carluccia told me. "Those who grew up on the land, with parents as farmers, do. There are a few that have remained in the countryside. But the small farmer basically doesn't exist anymore. She just doesn't exist. We are all but lost."

I spent the next few weeks unabashedly following Carluccia around everywhere she went. It turned out she was more farmer than cook, and that cooking was merely a natural extension of working the land. We spent time together in both the fields and her simple cooking hut. We

Carluccia cooks wild greens over an open fire in her cooking hut.

rolled pasta for hours, foraged for wild greens and spices, shelled beans, hung onions to dry, and picked strange fruits from old varieties of trees. We prepared lunches for the olive harvesters, and preserved vegetables for the shelves.

We were feeding the olive workers in the same way that Carluccia's grandmother fed the *paricchiu* years ago. In the past, when they didn't have enough hands to work the fields, they called in other farmers with their animals and plows to help. *Paricchiu* was the dialect term that referred to this whole package of labor. While the *paricchiu* worked the fields, planting or harvesting, Carluccia and her grandmother would prepare a special lunch of *filej*, fresh Calabrian pasta. It was just water and flour. We made it together on a few damp evenings, in a little shed off the fields.

Carluccia started by filling a plastic tub with soft flour. She poured a few glugs of water into the tub and began turning the flour and water together. Very quickly there was a thick goopy mass of dough coating her right hand. She continued folding it upon itself, again and again. "Watch the weather! If it's too humid outside, the dough gets soft and is hard to knead. If it's dry outside, and hard to incorporate the flour into the softer parts of the dough, sprinkle a little water with your hands over the pasta. Knead until it becomes smooth." She was leaning slowly and fully into the dough, rocking it rhythmically from side to side. This pasta was made from the hips.

Once the dough was smooth and springy to the touch of a thumb, Carluccia and I rolled it into thick ropes and then thinner strands. We tore the strands into segments about two inches long, and sprinkled them with a dusting of flour. Then, one by one, for a good hour, we twisted our little pasta worms around stalks of grain, and rolled them out in confident strokes. We ended up with hundreds of *filej*.

Rolling soft spirals of pasta was both pleasure and necessity for Carluccia. Pleasure in that the family and workers always loved a meal of *filej*, dressed with tomatoes, or beans, or herby greens, and olive oil. And necessity because it was too expensive to buy a lot of *pasta asciutta* (dried pasta). Her family had grown varieties of wheat for generations; it was freshly milled, inexpensive, and made delicious pastas and breads. As a family they had always been, and still were, almost

"As a family they had always been, and still were, almost totally self-sufficient."

Clockwise from top left: Carluccia's husband walking one of their cows. Carluccia rolling *filej*. Carluccia's cooking hut. Carluccia shelling butter beans and placing them in the *pignata*.

totally self-sufficient. Carluccia told me that the only things she buys are coffee, sugar, and salt. Even the soap she uses is made from last year's olive oil.

Given the wide variety of meats, fruits, and vegetables that the family produced, it was interesting to me that they didn't sell their products. Carluccia had only talked about her produce being used for the family itself, and their agritourism's guests. It was a touchy subject, and one that caused Carluccia visible dismay. Despite the area's deep history of subsistence farming, it appeared that this was now all but lost. There didn't even exist a viable marketplace for the local farmers. This had become particularly problematic in the selling and purchasing of meat—it was virtually impossible for a small farmer to sell his pastured beef, pork, or lamb, and even harder to buy. "You have to have a license now, you have to get papers from the veterinarian, and you have to have the animal slaughtered in a standard butcher shop, where they kill poorly raised animals. Besides, the butcher only pays you a pittance. These things don't have a price. It's just not worth all this to sell our beautiful animals for meat in that way."

It had been raining. The earth was heavy and wet. In a way this was good; it made pulling the plants out of the ground much easier. But all that water and gloppy earth also dirtied the beans, requiring more washing later on. We gathered enough plants to shell beans for lunch. This was going to be a very special meal, cooked by the fireside—beans in *pignatta*, and wild greens. A *pignatta* is a terra-cotta urn with a small handle on each side and a knobbed lid that rests on top. Carluccia remembered her grandmothers and great-grandmothers cooking the beans the same way, in the same terra-cotta *pignatte*.

At a certain point, Carluccia paused; she was talking about her hands again. She held them up for me to take a close look and said, "My hands are always in contact with the earth. But they're not ugly. Look at them . . . they're beautiful. Much better than those that touch toxins. Our land is clean, we don't use anything toxic. It's just natural soil." I looked at Carluccia's hands. Their skin was thick and old and caked with dirt. Her hands looked like moving earth. "If you don't pay attention to what you do," she added, "you'll ruin your hands."

Once we had shelled enough of the large white *fagioli di burro* for lunch, we washed up in an outdoor sink. This sink was magical. It was nestled gently behind a screen of trees where four fields converged. There was a good view out onto the olive groves, and to one of the fields of beans. Pomegranate trees hung their ruby-red fruits overhead, chickens clucked in a dirt-filled bathtub, and a moss-lined stone pond of water dripped slowly next to us. We washed the beans methodically, rubbing them together between our palms in buckets of fresh water.

> "I looked at Carluccia's hands. Their skin was thick and old and caked with dirt. Her hands looked like moving earth."

Carluccia's hands picking a rare variety of fruit from one of her trees.

As we worked side by side Carluccia told me she grew her butter beans on two plots of land that are within a stone's throw from each other. While the earth in these fields had very similar properties, the beans from one always had a richer, fuller flavor than those from the other. Carluccia knew this, and so cooked the milder ones with herbs or meat, to boost their taste. She also adjusted her cooking method according to the stage of the bean's maturation: If they were moist and plump in their pods, they cooked for a shorter amount of time, and if they were older and drier in the pod, they were soaked for a number of hours before being boiled in almost double the amount of water used for the plump ones. The beans could also be picked very early in the season, and eaten as green string beans. The year's weather, and the time of harvest, would yield different tastes and textures.

Clean beans and springwater went into the *pignatte*, and the *pignatte* went into the fire pit inside Carluccia's stone cooking hut. We made a fire from twigs, crumpled newspaper, and larger branches that Carluccia snapped into pieces over her right knee. Carluccia lit our fire with a laugh and a purple Bic lighter. Once the fire was going and the beans were off to a good start, we closed the door, left the smoke behind us, and headed back into the fields.

Whenever Carluccia made beans in *pignata*, she couldn't help but to go foraging for wild edible greens. She was hardwired in this way; shelling beans meant autumn, and autumn meant wild greens. She took me into a pasture, and from what looked to my naive eye like just another patch of grass, Carluccia began to pluck a variety of leafy plants. They were growing spontane-

ously, in clusters, and all it took to find them was a knowledgeable eye. Carluccia said that in Italy today "most young people don't go into the fields anymore to forage. They don't know how to recognize wild foods." The greens were particularly abundant at this time of year, when the rains had started and the temperatures were cooler. Their season had begun in October, and would last until May. By June, the earth would be too hot and dry, causing the plants to flower and seed, rendering them inedible.

We collected basketfuls of these exotic, mostly nameless greens. Carluccia described the unique properties and taste of each, although she always cooked them all together. The younger ones were the most tender and delicate in flavor. Others were quite bitter or almost creamy. Some were even sweet. The wild greens were more nutrient-dense than cultivated varieties, and the broth left over from boiling them was delicious and very good for the liver; drinking the mineral-rich cooking water was believed to remove toxins from the body. It was nature's way of cleaning us up.

Smoke billowed out of the cooking hut when we went to put on water for the greens. The *pignate* were frothing out of their tops, and we used twigs to scrape away this bean foam. Carluccia picked up the scalding hot pignate with her bare hands and shook them to mix the beans. They were almost done. The water came to a rolling boil for our wild greens, and we added them to the pot with a good dose of salt. A few minutes later we were all gathered at the table, eating beans, greens, and olive oil. It was one of the best meals I had in Italy, full of nature's elements; earth, fire, and water.

Carluccia taught me to pay attention to each little thing in my cooking. Where is this fruit or vegetable in its life cycle? Is the meat from a young animal or an older one? And what part of the animal is it from? Where are we in the season? Has the weather been damp or dry, sunny or cold lately? How fresh is the flour? Is the water hard or soft? What can I infer about my ingredient's flavor and texture? And who am I feeding? Are they happy, or in need of comfort? Are they cold to the bone from being out in the rain, or hot and sweaty? Ultimately, what is the most appropriate way for me to cook this food, to bring out the best it has to offer for my friends and family? Cooking became a matter of looking and listening carefully to my ingredients, and to the people who I am feeding.

Gathered *corbezzoli* fruits from Carluccia's land.

Carluccia : Zambrone, Calabria

Menu One

Filej with White Beans, Red Onion, and Raw Tomato
(Hand-Rolled Calabrian Pasta)

Roasted Broccoli Shoots with Olive Oil and Salt

Fichi Secchi Ripieni
(Dried Figs with Walnuts and Fennel Seeds)

Menu Two

Frittelle di Fiori di Zucca
(Fried Squash Blossom Bundles)

Braised Goat with Red Onions, Wild Fennel, and Juniper Berries

Erbe Selvatiche
(Wilted Wild Greens)

Nocino
(Walnut Liquor)

Walnut Black Pepper Cookies

Menu Three

Timpan di Patate
(Potato Pie with Prosciutto and Smoked Provola)

Peperoni al Forno
(Roasted Peppers with Garlic and Parsley)

Fennel and Lemon Salad

MENU ONE

Filej with White Beans, Red Onion, and Raw Tomato
(Hand-Rolled Calabrian Pasta)
Serves 4

Carluccia makes filej most often in the winter, when there are fewer daylight hours to work the fields; all the kneading and rolling brings the added benefit of warming the cook during the colder months. This is a recipe that should be made in the company of family or friends. The rolling of the spirals takes time, and the process becomes playful for a small group.

For the *filej*:
2 cups very fine semolina flour,
  or type 00 flour for pasta
10 tablespoons water, plus more in
  sprinkles if the dough starts to
  dry out

For the white beans, red onion,
  and raw tomato:
¼ cup olive oil
2 cup thinly sliced red onions or
  spring onions
½–1 teaspoon fresh minced
  peperoncino
½ teaspoon salt
3 cups cooked white beans
½ cup bean water
1 cup baby tomatoes, cut in half
¼ cup loosely packed fresh basil,
  chopped

Place the flour in a large mixing bowl, and make a well in the center of it. Add the 10 tablespoons of water and slowly mix into the flour, using your fingertips. Press the dough down and around again and again, until it coheres into a shaggy mass. At this point, turn the dough onto a lightly floured surface and begin to knead it. Feel free to sprinkle the dough with a little water if it is too dry to come together. Likewise, if the dough is too wet and sticky to knead, dust with a little flour. Knead for 20 minutes, until the dough is smooth and springs back to the pressing of a thumb.

Using the palms of your hands against the work surface, roll the dough into ropes about ¼ inch in diameter. Cut the ropes into strands about 2 inches long. Twist each strand tightly around a skewer, hay stalk, or small wire, and press down as you roll the pasta forward in one confident stroke. Remove the *filej* from the skewer and set aside on a lightly floured surface. Repeat the procedure with the rest of the dough.

Once all of the *filej* has been rolled, you can leave it out for a day to dry, or cook it right away. To cook the *filej* fresh, you will need to boil it for about 10 minutes in salted water to which a spoonful of olive oil has been added. Drying the pasta will require a longer cooking time, 16 to 20 minutes. The *filej* is done when it has softened but is still a little chewy to the bite. It is my preference to enjoy it immediately with spicy white beans, red spring onions, and lots of olive oil.

Warm the olive oil in a large sauté pan set over medium-low heat. Add the onions, *peperoncino*, and salt, and gently sauté them until the onions have softened and begun to caramelize. At this point, turn the flame down to low, and add the white beans and bean water. After a few minutes, when the cooking juices have started to come together, add the tomatoes and cook just until they are beginning to collapse a little. Turn off the heat, add the chopped basil, and toss with the *filej*. Serve with a little extra drizzle of olive oil, and a shaving of pecorino or Parmesan if desired.

Roasted Broccoli Shoots with Olive Oil and Salt
Serves 6–8 as a side dish

Carluccia grows many rows of broccoli on her land. Toward the end of the growing season the cut broccoli stems will put out wiry little shoots; these are delicious cooked in the same pot as the *filej*, or roasted, as they are here, for a crispy treat on the side.

> *2 pounds broccoli shoots or florets*
> *5 tablespoons olive oil*
> *1 teaspoon salt*

Preheat the oven to 450 degrees F.

Toss the broccoli with the olive oil and salt. Roast on two baking sheets for 12 to 15 minutes, or until crispy and browned.

Fichi Secchi Ripieni (Dried Figs with Walnuts and Fennel Seeds)

Serves 4–6

In the late summer and autumn, Carluccia lays out fresh figs to dry in the sun. She studs them with fennel seeds; as the fruits dry, they absorb the anise flavor of the fennel. We enjoyed them after lunch on many occasions, with pieces of Carluccia's freshly cracked walnuts.

> *12–15 dried figs*
> *½ teaspoon fennel seeds, crushed*
> *¼ cup lightly crushed walnuts*
> *⅓–½ pound fresh sheep's- or cow's-milk ricotta*
> *Local honey*

Cut the figs almost in half, leaving the stem portion uncut, so the figs remain joined at the top. Place on dessert plates, and sprinkle with fennel seeds and crushed walnut pieces. Spoon a little ricotta on the plate in a way that is pleasing to the eye. Drizzle with a touch of the local honey.

Menu Two

Frittelle di Fiori di Zucca (Fried Squash Blossom Bundles)
Serves 6

Carluccia made me these puffy bundles of fried squash blossoms for our first lunch together. Squash blossoms are luxurious in these *fritelle*, but they are also delicious when made with a wide variety of other vegetables; grated carrots, sautéed chard stems with garlic, or blanched cauliflower and broccoli all make great choices.

1–2 cups water
1 cup semolina flour
1 egg, lightly beaten
1 teaspoon salt
Generous amount of black pepper
2 cups squash flowers or 1 cup vegetables, cut small and blanched
Oil, for frying

To garnish:
1 tablespoon finely chopped fresh rosemary
Flaky sea salt
1–2 lemons, cut lengthwise into wedges

Add enough water into the flour to make a thick batter, whisking constantly. Beat in the egg, salt, and pepper. Add more water, as needed, to reach a consistency similar to that of a thick cake batter.

Gently fold the squash flowers into your batter. Heat the oil in a wide sauté pan until it starts to shimmer. Spoon large tablespoons of the batter with blossoms into the hot oil, and fry until lightly browned (about 2 minutes on each side). Remove with a slotted spoon, and lay to rest on layers of paper towel or brown paper bags. Garnish with a sprinkle of rosemary, and sea salt, if needed. Serve with a lemon wedge.

Braised Goat with Red Onions, Wild Fennel, and Juniper Berries

Serves 4–6

Carluccia raised goats on her farm for their milk and their meat. She taught me a great deal about the best ways to prepare goat, emphasizing that her preferred method was to tenderize the meat through slow, moist cooking. This recipe pays homage to Carluccia, to her pastured animals, and to the vibrant wild and cultivated herbs and spices growing around her property. It is rich with the aromas of fennel seeds and pollen, juniper berries, and fresh thyme and bay leaves, and pairs well with both Mary's Roasted Potatoes with Rosemary and Olive Oil, and Mamma Maria's Crushed Baby Potatoes with Lemon and Chives.

1½ cups red wine
2–3 pounds goat shoulder blade chops
Salt
3–4 tablespoons olive oil
2 cups minced red onions
4 cloves garlic, finely minced
½ cup minced celery
10 large sprigs fresh thyme
2 bay leaves
1 fresh or dried hot red pepper, finely minced
10 juniper berries, crushed finely using a
   mortar and pestle
½ teaspoon fennel seeds, crushed
2 tablespoons tomato paste
Water, as needed

To garnish:
Lemon juice
½ teaspoon wild fennel pollen
3 tablespoons chopped parsley

Place the red wine in a small saucepan, bring to a gentle boil, and simmer to reduce by half, 7 to 10 minutes. Turn off the heat and set aside.

Pat the meat dry and season it generously with salt. Heat 1½ tablespoons of olive oil in a heavy-bottomed pot set over medium-high heat until it shimmers. Add the meat (in batches if you need to) and brown both sides in the oil, about 10 minutes total for each batch. Remove the seared goat to a shallow dish and set aside.

Reduce the heat to medium-low and sauté the onions with a pinch of salt until just soft,

5 to 7 minutes. Feel free to add the remaining oil if the onions are sticking too much to the bottom of the pot. Add a pinch of salt, the garlic, celery, herbs, and crushed spices. Sauté for 5 to 7 minutes longer.

Return the goat and its juices to the pot, and add the wine, tomato paste, and ¾ cup of water. Bring to a slow boil and then reduce the heat to a gentle simmer. Cover with a lid set ever so slightly ajar, and cook for 1½ to 2 hours, adding more water if the sauce is becoming too thick for an easy, fluid simmer. Turn the meat over two or three times during its cooking; by the time it is done the liquid should have reduced to a thick and flavorful sauce. Remove the bay leaf and thyme sprigs. Add salt to taste, and a squeeze of lemon if you desire. Sprinkle with the fennel pollen and parsley immediately before serving.

Erbe Selvatiche (Wilted Wild Greens)
Serves 4–6 as a side dish

"Go forage for wild greens!" Carluccia would say. "Wherever you are, you're sure to find some. Or, even better, go and ask an elder to show you where they are." Wild is definitely best, but you can always make a delicious dish with a mixture of cultivated greens; Carluccia recommended a combination of spinach, arugula, dandelion greens, and chard. Though you can boil them on the stove, Carluccia believes that cooking them over firewood yields a taste that is more delicious and "elemental."

1 pound mixed wild or bitter greens, such as nettles and dandelions
2 tablespoons olive oil
½ lemon, juiced
Salt

Bring a large pot of salted water to a rolling boil. While you wait for the water to come to a boil, trim the cooking greens of the bottom of their stems, and wash them well.

Once the water is boiling, add the greens to the pot, return the water to a boil, and cook for 3 to 4 minutes.

Drain the greens and toss them with the olive oil and lemon juice. Taste for salt, adding more if you desire.

Nocino (Walnut Liquor)
Makes 2 liters of liquor

This process for making this walnut liquor is one of those very particular things that people really seem to believe in. According to Carluccia's neighbor, Enzo, in order to produce the best *nocino* you need to collect twenty-four fresh green walnuts at high noon on June 24, the day of San Giovanni. (He insists that at this precise date and time the Calabrian summer sun has evaporated the right amount of humidity from the walnuts and intensified their flavor, making for the perfect *nocino*.) As kooky as this sounds, I must admit that Enzo's walnut liquor was the best that I have ever tasted.

24 green walnuts
1 liter alcohol
10 cloves
2 cinnamon sticks
1 pound sugar
1 liter water

Shell and dry the walnuts, and clean them with a cloth (do not wash). Divide each walnut into eight pieces. (To do this, cut it in half first lengthwise, then widthwise. Finally, cut the walnut in half so that the two halves of the nut separate.) Place all of the walnut pieces in a widemouthed glass jar with a lid. Add the alcohol, cloves, and cinnamon sticks, and screw on the lid. Set the jar aside for 40 days, turning it once in the morning and once in the evening.

After the 40 days have passed, filter the mixture, setting aside the walnut and spice solids. Melt the sugar in the water, and add the sugar liquid to the alcohol. Set aside to cool. Place in a large glass bottle, seal well, and store in a cool dark place. After 2 years the *nocino* will be ready!

Walnut Black Pepper Cookies

Makes 2 dozen cookies

Carluccia loved the earthy, creamy taste of her land's walnuts; for this cookie I combined their flavor with one of her favorite spices, the black peppercorn, which we foraged for together along Calabria's wild coastline. The mixture of the peppercorns and walnuts with the butter and honey creates a light, nutty, and ever-so-slightly spicy tea cookie.

½ cup (1 stick) soft unsalted butter
3 tablespoons cane sugar
¾ teaspoon freshly ground black pepper
A pinch of salt
3 tablespoons semi-runny honey (I like a darker honey here—wildflower or chestnut)
1 cup (4 ounces) raw walnuts, pounded or coarsely ground
1 cup flour
Extra granulated sugar, for sprinkling the cookies

Preheat the oven to 300 degrees F. Line a baking sheet with parchment paper.

Cream the butter with the sugar until light and fluffy. Add the black pepper, pinch of salt, and honey; mix to incorporate. Add the nuts and flour, and mix with the electric mixer until the dough forms moist clumps, a few minutes.

Roll large teaspoonfuls of the batter between your clean hands, to make little balls. Place the balls on the baking sheet, and press down on them twice with the tines of a fork to make a crosshatch pattern. Sprinkle with a little bit of granulated sugar. Bake the cookies for 25 minutes, or until their bottoms have turned golden-nutty brown. Set aside to cool. For a complete walnut experience, enjoy the cookies with sipfuls of the following sweet walnut liquor.

Timpan di Patate (Potato Pie with Prosciutto and Smoked Provola)
Serves 8

Carluccia and her sister, Domenica, prepared this surprisingly easy and unique dish together for dinner one night. Think of this as being akin to a potato lasagna; it is rich and substantial, acting as an easy and affordable main course for many. Be sure to whip the egg whites before incorporating them, and if possible, use a potato ricer to sieve the potatoes; these two techniques contribute an important airiness to the richness of the pie.

5 pounds mashing potatoes
  (I use Yukon Gold)
1½ tablespoons salt, divided
1 cup milk, warmed
1½ sticks (¾ cup) butter,
  at room temperature
3 eggs, separated

½ pound smoked mozzarella or provola,
  cut into small pieces
⅓ pound thinly sliced prosciutto
3 ounces freshly grated Parmesan
3 whole eggs
½ cup bread crumbs

Preheat the oven to 375 degrees F, and butter a 9- by 13-inch rectangular baking dish.

Peel the potatoes, and cut them into quarters. Boil them in a pot of water with 1 tablespoon of the salt until soft (about 15 minutes). Press through a potato ricer, or mash well with a hand masher. Gently stir the warm milk, 1 stick of the butter cut into pieces, and the remaining salt into the warm potatoes. Whip the egg whites until they form soft peaks, and fold them in.

Place a layer of mashed potatoes about 1 inch high in the buttered dish. Dot the top with smoked cheese, then a single layer of prosciutto, and finally a generous sprinkling of Parmesan. Create another layer of potatoes, and top it with the cheeses and prosciutto (you should finish the smoked mozzarella and prosciutto on this layer, but make sure to reserve enough Parmesan for the final topping). Add a final layer of mashed potatoes, and dot with slivers of butter from the remaining ½ stick.

Whisk together the egg yolks with the 3 whole eggs. Pour this over the top of the potatoes. Sprinkle with the remaining Parmesan, and then the bread crumbs. Bake for about 40 minutes, or until the top of the potato pie has puffed up and turned a deep golden brown.

Peperoni al Forno (Roasted Peppers with Garlic and Parsley)
Serves 6–8

Carluccia roasts her peppers in a wood-burning oven as it is cooling down from the baking of bread. These delicious peppers keep well for a number of days, often even improving with time.

8 large, thick-fleshed peppers, washed and dried
1 clove garlic, very finely minced
2 tablespoons roughly chopped parsley
Salt to taste
¼ cup olive oil

Roast the peppers on a parchment-lined baking sheet for 25 minutes at 450 degrees F. Turn the peppers over, and roast for another 15 minutes, or until peppers have collapsed and started to blacken. Remove and set aside until they are cool enough to handle. Peel off the skins, remove the seeds and stems, and tear into strips. Sprinkle with garlic, parsley, and salt. Drizzle with olive oil.

Fennel and Lemon Salad
Serves 6–8

The fresh texture of shaved fresh fennel and lemon complement the richness of Carluccia's potato pie wonderfully, brightening and balancing the meal.

2 large or 4 small fennel bulbs, with fronds
1 small lemon, zested and juiced
Salt to taste
3 tablespoons olive oil
Freshly ground black pepper

Halve the fennel bulbs lengthwise, and carve out their woody bases. Slice the fennel as thinly as you can. Add the lemon juice to the shaved fennel, tossing well. Sprinkle with a little salt, drizzle on the olive oil, and toss again. Trim the fluffiest, youngest-looking fennel fronds off the stem, and mince finely (about ¼ cup). Sprinkle the fronds, lemon zest, and black pepper over the fennel.

Raffaela

Devi solo alimentarlo.

You just feed it.

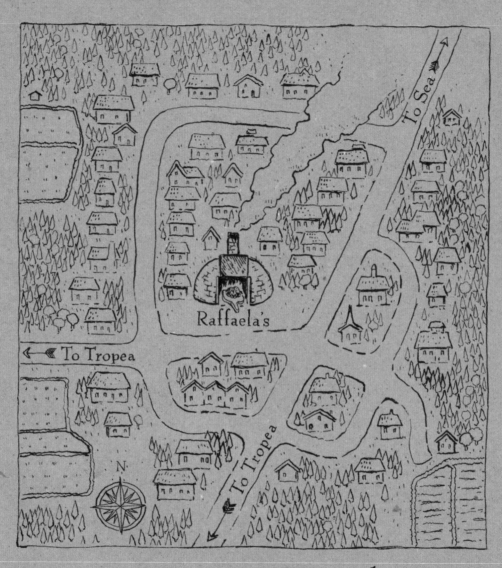

Raffaela's

To Sea

To Tropea

To Tropea

N.

Potenzoni, Calabria

Carluccia regularly made bread for her family. Truth be told, though, her children also bought bread from the local baker on a biweekly basis; in fact, everyone from miles around did. Carluccia would probably deny that Raffaela's bread was superior to hers, but even she occasionally gave in to Raffaela's ethereal loaves.

In times past, the villages around Tropea had a highly refined system of breadmaking. Each woman would take a turn in feeding the communal clump of wet, naturally yeasty starter. She would mix and knead a sourdough, then fire up her wood-burning oven to bake a batch of bread that would feed not only her own family, but those of the other women in the town. In this way, everyone always had fresh bread daily, and no one woman had to work too hard to put it on her table. It was collaborative and efficient, providing the Italian staff of life, uniquely infused with the local land's beneficial yeasts and bacteria.

By the time I arrived in Calabria, these elegantly orchestrated, traditional bread ways had disappeared. The older generation of women was dwindling, and most of the region's young people had moved to the north of Italy, where there was work and money to be found. Besides, bread could now be bought from the supermarket, and while such bread did not contain the tradition or health benefits of the historic sourdough, it still served its basic, sauce-slopping purpose.

Rose gave me half a loaf of Raffaela's bread upon my arrival at Pirapora. It was a revelation; I had never tasted anything so chewy, crunchy, and airy, slightly sour, slightly sweet. It was the best bread I had ever eaten, and I needed to learn how to make it. Rose took me for an introduction, and Raffaela agreed that I should come the next time she made bread, two mornings later.

I quickly learned that baking bread was akin to tending a young child; Raffaela had to feed her dough daily with flour and water, and although she only baked on Tuesdays and Fridays, most of her free time was spent attending to the process. Simply preparing the dough took a full day and a half. First Raffaela made a liquid sponge from the starter, letting it ferment and thicken for a number of hours. She then mixed and kneaded a pliable dough, which took almost a day to rise and double. Finally, she stretched, cut, and shaped the dough into loaves, and set them under clean sheets and wool blankets for one final rest before they were slashed quickly with a knife and plunged into the scalding-hot, ashen oven.

Many of the steps in making Raffaela's bread necessitated work in the wee hours of the night. The townspeople from all around began arriving at 8 a.m. to pick up their piping-hot loaves. This meant that the dough needed to have had its final rest for at least a few hours before going into the oven at 6:30 a.m., all of which often required a 2 a.m. stretch and shape. Additionally, the coastal Calabrian weather varied greatly between summer and winter, constantly changing the dough's feeding and rising needs. When the ambient temperature was cool, the bread took longer to rise; when it was hot, fermentation often progressed too rapidly and the dough needed to be closely monitored. Raffaela's life and schedule were dependent on the whims of the sun and clouds, the rain and the heat. For the bread to remain consistent, she had to constantly take the pulse of all this, making informed and intuitive decisions accordingly.

The art of naturally leavened breadmaking was difficult for me to grasp at first, and I only fully understood it much later, after piecing together my observations of Raffaela with my sourdough experiments stateside. At the end of the first morning, Raffaela tore off a sticky knob of

"The townspeople from all around began arriving at 8 a.m. to pick up their piping-hot loaves."

Left: Raffaela's wood-burning oven just after the loaves have been placed inside.
Opposite: A view of the local Calabrian coast, olive trees, and a rainbow on a stormy day.

her dough and handed it to me, insisting that I bake with it in America. There, my native air could contribute its mixture of yeasts to hers, creating a unique Italian American bread. The only concrete instructions she gave me were to feed it with flour, and to give it a very hot bake.

Each morning, while Raffaela's daughter assisted her faithfully and quietly, her chatterbox son Domenico managed the fire needed to heat the oven for the bread. I was highly amused by this man's compulsive, almost tic-like overuse of the word *magari* ("maybe" or "perhaps"), and he was equally fascinated by me and my impressions of both Calabria and America. In an offering of friendship, he insisted on taking me on a driving tour of the area.

Domenico gave me an odd perspective on the region's highlights, which consisted of a couple of stops at crumbling, abandoned towns. These were akin to the tiny deserted hamlets I had walked by in Lunigiana, but on a significantly larger scale. They were fully formed, previously flourishing, medium-size towns. The ancient stone buildings had been inhabited for centuries, until the postwar depressions hit the south of Italy, propelling its youth both northward and over land and sea to more affluent countries. With the working young transplanted to richer lands, the remaining local commerce and industry stagnated. The elders and their towns languished and died together, as their grandchildren sent them money in envelopes from distant regions and countries. The people and traditional cultures of these small towns simply evaporated, leaving behind an eerie atmospheric hint at what had once been. This was a raw, rough land, one in which few had escaped the mark of severe financial deprivation and the money-hungry Calabrian mafia. It was no wonder that Mamma Maria and Giovanna had been so protective of me when I had spoken of traveling to the south of Italy alone; they were safeguarding my soft, youthful naïveté.

After my last morning of baking with Raffaela she invited me upstairs, into her home, for coffee. She took off her baker's cap to reveal a bundle of dark hair; despite her long life, she still had the strong air of youth. As we dunked dry *biscotti* into sweet *espresso*, Raffaela talked briefly about her husband dying young, leaving her a widow with six children. Poverty-stricken and in the middle of the rural south, she had no idea how to support her family. And then she remembered the bread from her childhood, how it had survived through the hands of many generations. She needed to make that bread; it represented something wholesome and good, something lasting that would otherwise be lost. With that she had renovated her oven, found a scrap of her ancestors' sourdough starter, and begun to bake. The people came in droves.

Raffaela dusting her loaves of bread with flour before baking.

RAFFAELA : POTENZONI, CALABRIA

BREAD

The Town Sourdough Bread

Sourdough Pancakes with *Marmellata*

Calabrian Bread Salad

Fresh Breadcrumbs

The Town Sourdough Bread

Sourdough Starter

Maintaining and baking with a sourdough starter is akin to having a pet. The starter needs to be fed regularly, and truly each starter has a character and style of its own when it comes to baking. The simplest way to obtain a sourdough starter is from friends or acquaintances at the time they are replenishing theirs; such established starters are desirable in that the yeasts have a sturdiness that is developed through time and symbiosis with the local environment. That said, it is also quite simple to build a sourdough starter from scratch. Starter particularly likes to begin its life in a warm and well-used kitchen—the kind that has organic fruits and vegetables ripening in it. Once you establish your starter, I recommend that you store and feed it in a wide-mouthed quart-size mason jar.

1½ cups flour (preferably freshly milled)
1½ cups filtered water (or water from boiling potatoes or pasta)

Make sure that your flour and water are at room temperature. In a medium-size bowl, vigorously stir together the flour and water for a few minutes. Cover with cheesecloth or a clean and porous cloth. Set aside in a warm (70 to 80 degrees F) and well-ventilated part of your kitchen, preferably near some ripening fruits or vegetables. Vigorously stir the mixture a few times a day, for 3 to 5 days, until small bubbles appear naturally on the surface of the starter. If bubbles have not appeared after 4 or 5 days, try adding a couple of organic grapes to the batter and moving it to a warmer spot.

After bubbles have begun to appear on the surface of the starter, feed it 2 tablespoons of flour and 1 tablespoon of water each day for 3 to 4 consecutive days. Continue to vigorously stir the starter a few times each day during this time, leaving it covered with the cheesecloth at room temperature. Once your starter is thick and bubbly, it is ready to use. To keep the starter alive and active, you will need to maintain and refresh it on a regular basis. If you store your starter at room temperature, you need to feed it daily; otherwise the starter can be kept in the refrigerator and fed weekly. In the latter case, remember to leave it out at room temperature for 4 to 8 hours of bubbling before you return it to the fridge. This will allow the yeasts time to replenish before slowing down in the refrigerator.

To refresh your starter and prepare it for baking, pour off all but ¼ cup of it. (Now would be a good time to make sourdough pancakes with the starter that you remove.) Feed the remaining ¼ cup of starter with ½ cup water and ¾ cup flour (preferably a high-protein bread flour). Leave out at room temperature for 8 to 12 hours.

After 8 to 12 hours, repeat the above procedure, discarding all but ¼ cup of the starter, and feeding the remaining starter with ½ cup filtered water and ¾ cup flour. Set aside for another 8 hours; after this fermentation period, the starter should be ready to use. Feeding the starter twice before making the sponge for bread ensures that the starter is lively enough to create well-risen bread. If your starter is not very actively bubbly, you can repeat this procedure a third or even a fourth time before going on to make your sponge.

Sourdough Bread

Makes 2 round loaves

What follows is the technique that I have developed to create delicious sourdough loaves with either Raffaela's starter or the native San Franciscan one that I have also been baking with recently. As with all naturally cultured foods, the starter and its baking times are sensitive to the temperature and humidity; this "recipe" was developed at an ambient temperature of roughly 70 degrees F. If humidity is high, you will need to use more flour or less water in the dough. If it's very dry where you live, you may need to add more water or less flour. Please be sure to use filtered or bottled water when baking with sourdough; the chlorine commonly found in tap water will kill off some of the important yeasts in the dough.

For the sponge:
¾–1 cup refreshed starter
½ cup filtered water
1 cup bread flour (high protein flour)

For the dough:
Sponge from above
1½ cups filtered water
2½ teaspoons fine sea salt
4–4½ cups bread flour (high protein flour)
Olive oil

Extra equipment:
Baking stone
Baking sheet
Razor blade
Parchment Paper

To make the sponge, stir together the refreshed starter and water in a large bowl. Whisk in the flour. Cover and set aside at room temperature until roughly doubled in size, about 3 hours.

To make the dough, whisk together the sponge with the water and the salt. Then, using a large wooden spoon, slowly mix in ½ cup of the flour at a time. Once you have added all the flour, knead the dough in the bowl until it comes together as a ball, 2 to 3 minutes. Cover and set aside to rest for half an hour.

Knead the dough on a clean surface for 12 to 15 minutes, until it becomes a firm ball. Coat a large, clean bowl with olive oil. Place the dough inside the bowl, and rub its surface with a little olive oil, too. Cover the dough tightly with plastic wrap. Set aside until it doubles in size again, typically 4 to 6 hours.

Turn the dough onto a clean surface, and cut it in half. Stretch out each lump of dough, and then fold it in thirds, over itself. Shape each loaf into a taut ball, pinching the bottom together to form a central seam. Place the dough on a baking sheet that has been lined with lightly floured parchment paper. Rub the dough with a touch more olive oil, and cover loosely with plastic wrap. Place in the fridge for the final rising, 8 to 12 hours.

When you are ready to bake the bread, take it out of the fridge and preheat your oven to 500 degrees F. If you have a baking stone, preheat it in the oven also. When the oven is up to temperature, slash the rounds of bread with a razor blade or sharp knife. Slide the baking sheet with the bread into the hot oven, and immediately toss a small glassful of water onto the bottom shelf of the oven. While this sounds somewhat outrageous, I find the technique to produce a much more crispy and puffy loaf than the alternative of spritzing the loaves with water. Bake until the loaves are a dark golden brown on the outside, and sound hollow when tapped on the bottom, 30 to 40 minutes. Transfer to a wire rack to cool.

Sourdough Pancakes with *Marmellata*

Serves 4

Feeding my sourdough starter creates the perfect excuse for making a batch of sourdough pancakes. To avoid creating an ever-expanding jar of starter, each time I replenish my sourdough (usually weekly), I remove a good portion of the bubbly liquid, turning it into a loaf of bread, sourdough crackers, or pancakes. I love the slightly sour taste the starter imparts, and also the increased digestibility that it provides through the naturally occurring local yeasts. These pancakes are delicious served with butter and a homemade *marmellata* (marmalade), jam, or compote.

½ cup cream or whole milk
1 tablespoon local honey
2 eggs
1 cup thick, but pourable, sourdough starter
½ cup flour (roughly)
½ teaspoon baking soda
Large pinch of salt
Butter, to grease the pan
Marmellata, jam, or compote and extra butter, to serve with the pancakes

In a medium-large bowl, whisk together the milk, honey, and eggs. Whisk in the sourdough, and add enough flour to make a thick but pourable batter (this should be about ½ cup, but feel free to add more or less if the batter looks like it needs to be thickened or thinned out). Stir in the baking soda and the large pinch of salt.

Heat a knob of butter (about a tablespoon) in a skillet or griddle set over medium heat. When the butter is fully melted and swirling hot, add a couple of ladlefuls of batter to the pan. Turn the burner down to medium-low, and cook the pancakes until bubbles cover the exposed side. Flip and cook on the other side until cooked through, and golden brown on the bottom.

Repeat this procedure, adding more butter between batches, to use all of the batter. I recommend serving the pancakes in batches, hot off the griddle, with a touch of butter and a spoonful of *marmellata* or jam.

Calabrian Bread Salad

Throughout Italy, it is common to find bread salads prepared with dry, leftover loaves. Less common, but in my opinion more delicious, is the taste of toasted, fresh bread incorporated into a ripe vegetable salad. Here, large chunks of bread are tossed with olive oil and roasted until crispy in the oven, then added to a typical Tropean salad made from tomatoes, red onions, peppers, and basil.

½ cup very thinly sliced red onion
1–2 tablespoon red wine vinegar (15 minute maceration)
¾ pound cherry tomatoes
1 green bell pepper
½ teaspoon very finely diced fresh hot red pepper
6 tablespoons olive oil, divided
½ teaspoon salt, divided
⅓ pound crustless artisan sourdough bread (about ½ loaf)
1 large garlic clove, peeled
A small handful of fresh basil leaves

Preheat your oven to 450/475 degrees F.

Mix the onions and vinegar together in a large bowl. Set aside to macerate for 10–20 minutes, to soften the pungency of the onions. While the onions are macerating, prepare the other ingredients for the bread salad.

Wash the cherry tomatoes, and slice them lengthwise into quarters. Wash the green pepper, and de-stem and seed it. Tear the green pepper into very small, bite-size pieces. Add the tomatoes, green pepper, and diced hot pepper, 3 tablespoons of the olive oil, and ¼ teaspoon of salt to the onion mixture. Stir to combine.

Tear the bread into 1-inch cubes, and toss it with the clove of garlic and the remaining 3 tablespoons of olive oil and ¼ teaspoon of salt. Spread out on a baking sheet and roast in the oven until lightly browned and crunchy on the outside, 15 to 25 minutes. Remove the clove of garlic and let the bread cool slightly before mixing with the salad.

Ten to fifteen minutes before serving, add the bread and a small handful of torn basil to the vegetable mixture. The bread will absorb some of the juices from the vegetables, allowing it to slightly soften, creating a crunchy-chewy texture.

Fresh Breadcrumbs

Yield depends on quantity of bread used

Breadcrumbs are great to have on hand, and are an integral part of many of the recipes I learned to cook in Italy. While they are delicious prepared with fresh bread, I find that the most appropriate time to make them is with leftover bread that is a few days old. Prepared then, the bread crumbs become a thrifty way to make the most of a product that is just past its prime.

1 loaf plain or sourdough bread, fresh or slightly old

Preheat the oven to 300 degrees F.

Slice the crusts off the bread and cut it into pieces. Shred the bread into small pieces, either by hand or by processing it in a food processor with an S blade. Spread the shredded bread evenly on an edged baking sheet. Bake for 20 to 25 minutes, tossing the crumbs and redistributing halfway through the cooking. The crumbs are done when they feel dry and crispy to the touch; they shouldn't turn more than a light golden brown. Set aside to cool, then store in an airtight container in the fridge for up to a month.

Maddalena

Fai attenzione. Potrebbe bruciarti.

Be careful. It could burn you.

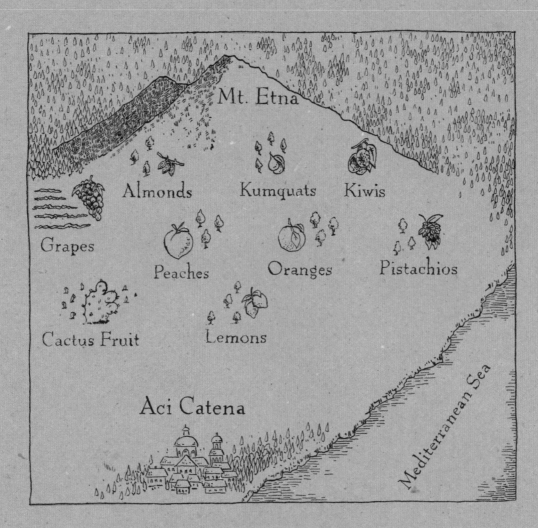

Mt. Etna

Grapes   Almonds   Kumquats   Kiwis

Peaches   Oranges   Pistachios

Cactus Fruit   Lemons

Aci Catena

Mediterranean Sea

Etna, Sicilia

My arrival at Maddalena's apartment foretold the rest
of my time with her. I rang the doorbell and Maddalena's husband opened the door with a loud
welcome and a big, wide smile. Maddalena appeared behind him, half obscured, in delicate silence.
We shook hands, and her husband showed me into the apartment and began talking about what
Maddalena was going to cook that day.

Maddalena's apartment was tiny. The kitchen was a makeshift area walled off on one end of
the balcony; it was humble, yet perfectly organized and surprisingly functional. From that kitchen
she turned out dishes exquisite in taste and technique. Crunchy almond caramels were made at the
speed of light with unsurpassed deftness, and fresh sardines were gently gutted and butterflied
with an easy slice, pull, and press. Maddalena was a modest, gifted cook. She used the products of
her local land and sea in just the right way to best highlight their flavor and tradition.

During that first lunch I learned about Mount Etna: Etna-the-volcano, snowy-topped-Etna
rising from a hot land, with an even hotter molten core. Etna, after whom Maddalena's city was
named. Understanding Etna explains certain aspects of the Sicilian personality. She is an active
volcano, typically sending out little eruptions of scorching lava daily, such that I saw patches of
glowing red in the distance at night. From time to time Etna really erupts. The Sicilians seemed
this way to me, too: just barely composed, hot as fire in parts, icy cold at times, simultaneously
distant and uncomfortably close. Life felt full-throttle and unpredictable to me in Sicily.

The Sicilians have always been drawn to growing their vegetables on the fertile, mineral-
rich volcanic soils of Etna. They edge up next to danger, knowing that this is where the most productive terrain lies. That soil, on that mountain, is known throughout the country to be the best in
Italy for fruit and nut trees. It's a big gamble, though. The trees take years to be fully productive,

and the threat of a major eruption is constant. One's plantings can be destroyed in an instant at Etna's whim. It has happened before. Still, her soil produces an unsurpassed depth in flavor and while all Italians love their food, the Sicilians really love their food, and in particular their sweets. Etna provides plenty to those living close to her. It is a dicey relationship.

Maddalena's husband told of how *granita* is reputed to have been "discovered" on the slopes of Etna, directly above Maddalena's town. I loved the image of those daring Sicilians growing their most flavorful fruits on Etna's slopes, packing their precious peaches in ice to carry down, delighted to find that some of the extra-ripe ones had crushed into the ice for a delicious treat. Maddalena's husband also told me that *gelato* was invented there, and it makes complete sense: One must find something to do with all those rich volcanic pistachios, lemons, prickly pears, hazelnuts, almonds, cherries, and oranges. What better than making a creamy frozen treat?

This was how most of my time was spent with Maddalena: Her husband stood forward, presenting stories, presenting food. And Maddalena stood back, turned toward the stove, hot but composed over frying eggplant and scalding caramel sugar. He lingered throughout the cooking, talking about the ingredients of the local area, and answering the questions I posed. When the cooking was over, he would proudly hold the food for my camera.

While I was not allowed to help Maddalena with the cooking and didn't get to interact with her directly during it, we did exchange some quiet conversation after lunch. As we thumbed through her books of meticulously kept family recipes, she gave a few details: how she had learned about candying by her grandmother's side, how a great-aunt was very good at making fish and her recipes were the best for it. Little things like that. She was unusually generous during our time with the books, opening them up carefully and eagerly offering to copy out or cook whichever recipes took my fancy. What struck me in these brief discussions was the boldness of the Sicilian

"From time to time Etna really erupts. The Sicilians
seemed this way to me, too: just barely composed,
hot as fire in parts, icy cold at times, simultaneously
distant and uncomfortably close."

Atop the volcanic Mount Etna, near Maddalena's home.

> "She was the devoted mother, the perfect homemaker,
> the exquisite cook, the available grandmother, the kind wife—
> and she was nearly voiceless."

palate. The flavors are forceful to begin with, and then the cook tends to boost them further with a heavy hand of sugar, spice, and salt. Maddalena's cooking was bright in these ways; she used strong-tasting vegetables like peppers and eggplant, salty capers and olives, acidic lemons and oranges, and sweet sprinklings of sugar.

Despite my relentless questions, Maddalena's history, her personality, remained strangely elusive to me. I took photographs of her, and yet I barely caught a glimpse of who she really was. Her physique was nonspecific in many ways; she was an average height, of medium build, with brown eyes and hair. And her history was so filtered by her husband and her silence that it was hard to grasp. In a way it was her lack of story that caught my attention.

Maddalena presented the archetype of the common traditional Italian woman, mother, grandmother, wife. She played a specific well-rehearsed role in her marriage and in the structure of her family and Italian society. She was the devoted mother, the perfect homemaker, the exquisite cook, the available grandmother, the kind wife—and she was nearly voiceless. She was a kind of dying Italian icon. It made me wonder about the impact of larger social structures; how in Italy everything had its place, for better or worse, and people knew their position within the grand scheme of things and inhabited it well. In many ways it felt repressive, but in certain ways there was a kind of freedom that came from not questioning one's role in life. It was hard for me to imagine.

Clockwise from top left: Maddalena prepares her almond *croccante*. A view towards the ocean from Maddalena's rooftop. Maddalena's husband serves her *croccante*. Vegetables and tomatoes simmering on Maddalena's stove for her *caponata*.

MADDALENA : ETNA, SICILIA

MENU ONE

Sarde a Baccafico
(Fresh Sardines with Bread Crumbs, Currants, and Olives)

Spaghetti con Pomodori Scoppiati
(Spaghetti with Burst Tomatoes)

Croccante di Mandorla
(Crunchy Almond Caramels)

MENU TWO

Panelle
(Chickpea Flour Fritters)

Grilled Tuna with Coriander and Mint

La Caponata
(Fried Vegetables in a Tomato Sauce)

Blood Orange *Gelato*

Menu One

Sarde a Baccafico (Fresh Sardines with Bread Crumbs, Currants, and Olives)
Serves 8–10 as an appetizer

This is Maddalena's version of the popular Sicilian dish of stuffed, roasted fresh sardines. Part of this recipe's tradition lies in preparing the sardines correctly; here they are butterflied open, filled with a sweet, herby bread filling, and rolled up to resemble dive-bombing birds. Fresh anchovies also work well in this dish.

24 fresh sardines or anchovies
2 tablespoons olive oil
½ red onion, finely minced
1 clove garlic
½ pound bread crumbs
3 tablespoons roughly chopped green olives
1 tablespoon currants

2 tablespoons minced fennel fronds or dill
2 tablespoons minced parsley
¼ cup grated Parmesan or hard pecorino
1½ lemons, juiced
Salt
Pepper
Bay leaves (optional)

Preheat the oven to 350 degrees F. Oil a small baking dish.

To prepare the sardines, cut off their heads and slit each fish's belly with a small sharp knife. Remove the innards, and flush the insides of the fish under cold running water. While the water is running, gently rub the fish from tail to head to remove the scales. Remove the central bone, leaving the top ridge of the fish intact so that it can be opened like a book. Press the fillets gently open so that their shape resembles that of a butterfly. Rinse again in water, and dry with a paper towel. Store in the refrigerator until the filling is ready.

Warm the olive oil in a skillet set over medium-low heat. Sauté the onion and garlic in the oil until they are soft. Add the bread crumbs and stir frequently to toast them lightly in the onion-oil mixture. Turn off the heat and stir in the green olives, currants, fennel fronds, parsley, Parmesan, the juice of 1 lemon, and salt and pepper to taste. Pat the sardines dry and lay them open flat, skin-side down. Place a tablespoon of the bread crumb filling on the head end of the sardine, and roll up toward the tail. Pack the sardines closely together, tail-side up, in the baking dish. Place a bay leaf between each sardine, if desired. Drizzle with a little olive oil and the remaining lemon juice.

Bake for 15 to 20 minutes.

Spaghetti con Pomodori Scoppiati (Spaghetti with Burst Tomatoes)
Serves 4

One of the most beloved and traditional Sicilian ingredients is *estrattu*, a slowly sun-dried tomato paste. For this dish, *estrattu* is added to a sauce made from seared, just bursting cherry tomatoes. This is a quick but beautifully layered pasta dish; the fresh and the preserved tomatoes marry well to create surprising complexity. I have found that a quick substitute for *estrattu* is to mince or puree oil-cured sun-dried tomatoes.

1 pound (2 pints) ripe cherry tomatoes
½ cup olive oil
5 large cloves garlic, finely minced
1 peperoncino, finely minced
⅓ cup finely minced oil-preserved
  sun-dried tomatoes
1 pound spaghetti
Salt to taste

For the garnish:
Small handful of torn fresh basil leaves
Grated Parmesan or hard pecorino

Bring a large pot of salted water to a boil for the pasta.

Wash the cherry tomatoes, and cut half of them in half. In a large sauté pan, heat the olive oil over medium-high heat. When the oil starts to shimmer, toss in the cherry tomatoes (both whole and halved), finely minced garlic, and hot pepper. The tomatoes should crackle and hiss upon hitting the oil. Sauté over high heat for 7 to 10 minutes, until the cut tomatoes start to flop and the whole ones look as if they are going to burst. Add the sun-dried tomatoes, and stir together for a minute to combine. Turn off the heat.

Boil the spaghetti until *al dente*, then drain. Place the sauté pan full of tomatoes back over high heat, and add the spaghetti. Toss to combine, and cook together for a minute to make the sauce cling to the noodles. Add salt to taste, sprinkle with torn basil, and serve with grated Parmesan or hard pecorino.

Croccante di Mandorla (Crunchy Almond Caramels)
Serves 10

Making crunchy caramels is another one of those techniques that seems complex, but Maddalena and her recipe make it very straightforward. Maddalena prepared her almond-filled brittles on a marble slab and served them with the bright green Bronte pistachios that are grown on Etna's slopes.

8¾ ounces almonds (about 1¾ cups)
1 lemon
10½ ounces white sugar (just shy of 1½ cups)

Optional garnishes:
2 tablespoons raw chopped pistachios
Flaky sea salt

Lay out a piece of marble, if you have one. Otherwise, place a large piece of parchment paper on your countertop.

Toast the almonds at 350 degrees F until fragrant, 10 to 12 minutes. Set aside to cool, and then chop them into very small pieces by hand or in the food processor; set them in a bowl next to your stovetop. Cut the lemon in half crosswise; juice one of the halves, and set aside the other for the final stage of the caramel procedure. Place 2 teaspoons of lemon juice and all of the sugar in a nonstick skillet. Heat the mixture over a low flame until it has completely melted, about 10 to 12 minutes. During this time, swirl the mixture to combine, but do not stir. Be very careful during the heating of the sugar—it will go from underdone to burned very, very quickly.

According to Maddalena, the best way to control the temperature and consistency of the caramel is to swirl it away from the flame toward the end of the melting sugar stage. Additionally, you want to stir in the almonds as soon as you see the following: The sugar has completely melted, and the caramel is turning from light to dark golden brown. When you see this, turn off the heat, quickly stir in the almonds, and pour the mixture onto the marble or parchment paper.

Use the other half of the cut lemon to spread the almond mixture out evenly and to flatten it to the thickness you desire (I recommend roughly ¼ inch thick). Work very quickly at this stage, as the mixture becomes unworkable within a minute.

Use a long sharp knife to cut the brittle immediately; first into long strips and then crosswise to form rectangles. Remove from the marble or parchment paper to a cooling rack or platter to cool and firm up.

For a special presentation, sprinkle the *croccante* with the raw pistachios or a light dusting of flaky sea salt, then serve on citrus leaves.

Menu Two

Panelle (Chickpea Flour Fritters)
Serves 6–8 as an appetizer

These piping-hot chickpea flour chips are a classic Sicilian appetizer; they are quite unusual, dead-easy to make, and immensely satisfying. I like the crispy chips both deep-fried, and more simply, pan-fried in a little olive oil. They are delicious served plain, with a sprinkling of salt, but also work well as the base for various toppings. Sicilian olive tapenade makes a perfect accompaniment.

3¼ cups water
½ pound chickpea flour
1½–2 teaspoons salt
Freshly ground black pepper
2 tablespoons minced fresh herbs, such as parsley, cilantro, or oregano
Seed oil, for frying

Place the water in a saucepan. Slowly whisk in the chickpea flour, making sure that lumps do not develop. Add salt and pepper to taste, and then place the saucepan over medium heat, stirring the mixture constantly with a wooden spoon. When the mixture has thickened to a polenta-like consistency, stir in the minced fresh herbs, remove it from the heat and, using a spatula, spread a thin layer of dough (⅛ to ¼ inch thick) onto a dinner plate or the back of a baking sheet. Once the dough has cooled, remove it from the surface by first going under it with a knife and then peeling it off. Cut it into long, thin triangles.

In a large sauté pan, heat about 2 inches of seed oil, and then fry the triangles in batches, making sure to turn them so that they are evenly browned on each side. You can tell when they are done because they turn golden brown and puff up slightly.

Place the *panelle* on paper towels to dry the excess oil off, and serve immediately. Caution: They are delicious . . . and hot!

Grilled Tuna with Coriander and Mint

Serves 4

As we ate our lunch, Maddalena's husband told me the story of Sicily's *mattanza*—the annual tuna massacre. Each summer, schools of migrating bluefin tuna pass along Sicily's west coast to be trapped in nets and finally hand-speared in an intense and ancient male ritual. The housewives along the coast then spend weeks oil-curing and grilling their men's catch. This grilled tuna dish makes use of dried spices, fresh herbs and citrus, and relies on the freshest of fish. I particularly recommend pairing it with Maddalena's *caponata*.

2 teaspoons coriander seeds
1 teaspoon fennel seeds
½–⅔ cup olive oil, divided
4 tuna steaks, each about 6 ounces
    and ¾" thick
Salt

Black pepper
¼ cup minced fresh dill
3 tablespoons minced fresh mint
1½ teaspoons finely minced or grated
    organic orange zest
1 lemon, cut into wedges, for garnish

Lightly toast the coriander and fennel seeds in a small skillet set over medium-low heat, 3 to 4 minutes. Remove the seeds from the heat immediately and crush them in a pestle and mortar, or a clean spice or coffee grinder. Mix the ground spices together with 1½ tablespoons of the olive oil.

Rinse the tuna under cold water and pat it dry. Sprinkle the tuna steaks generously with salt and pepper on both sides, and rub thoroughly with the spiced oil.

Warm a tablespoon of oil in a large skillet set over medium-high heat. When the surface of the oil starts to shimmer, add two of the tuna steaks to the pan. Sear the tuna for 2 to 3 minutes on the first side, until lightly browned. Flip the steaks and sear the other side for 2 to 3 minutes, depending on the thickness of the tuna. Check the tuna after 2 minutes by cutting into it. The above method and timing will cook the tuna so that it is still a little rare in the middle when you take it off the stove; it will continue to cook once removed from the heat and will be just pink at the time of serving. If you prefer a more rare-seared tuna, simply sear it for less time on each side.

In a small bowl, stir together the minced fresh dill and mint, the orange zest, and the remaining olive oil (about ⅓ to ½ cup). Add a sprinkle of salt to taste. To serve, drizzle the tuna with the herb-orange oil and accompany with a wedge of lemon.

La Caponata (Fried Vegetables in a Tomato Sauce)
Serves 4

Maddalena's *caponata* is shockingly good. She deep-fries eggplant, peppers, and potatoes, and then simmers them in a fresh tomato sauce. The result is a bright and flavorful dish that I like to think of as the Sicilian approach to ratatouille. Do not be off-put by the idea of deep-frying the vegetables here; the technique is very simple, and the texture and flavor surprisingly light.

For the tomato sauce:
1 tablespoon olive oil
½ red onion, finely minced
1 large clove garlic, finely minced
1½ pounds fresh tomatoes, roughly chopped
½ teaspoon finely minced fresh peperoncino (or ⅛ teaspoon dried hot pepper flakes)
¼ cup water
1½ teaspoons salt
Generous pinch of sugar
¼ cup fresh orange juice, stirred in at the end
Salt

For the vegetables:
1 liter (about 1 quart) high-heat vegetable oil, for frying
¾ pound yellow waxy potatoes, peeled and medium dice
¾ pound eggplant, medium dice
½ pound red bell pepper, medium dice

To prepare the tomato sauce, heat the olive oil in a large sauté pan set over medium heat. Add the minced red onion and garlic, and sauté until softened and turning golden, about 10 minutes. Add the tomatoes, hot pepper, water, salt, and large pinch of sugar. Bring the tomatoes to a simmer and cook for 15 minutes. Then add the fried vegetables, prepared according to the following directions.

Bring the vegetable oil up to heat in a heavy-bottomed pot (I use a 3½-quart enameled cast-iron pot for this). Ideally, you want the temperature to hover around 325 degrees F; it should take 6 to 7 minutes with the pot of oil set over medium heat to get it there. Another way to tell when the oil is hot enough for frying is by dropping one of the potatoes into the oil; it should froth and bubble instantly, and take 3 to 4 minutes to cook through without burning. Once the oil has arrived at temperature, use a slotted spoon to lower in a batch of potatoes. Fry until golden brown and cooked through, turning the vegetables from time to time with a slotted spoon. Strain the potatoes from the oil and add them to the tomato sauce. Repeat this procedure to fry all of the vegetables, modulating the oil temperature by turning the heat up or down to create an even fry. I recommend frying the potatoes first, followed by the eggplant, and finally the red peppers. The eggplant and peppers will take less time to cook than the potatoes; be sure to add the freshly fried vegetables into the simmering tomato sauce as soon they are done.

Once all of the vegetables have been added, continue to cook the sauce long enough for the ingredients to come together into a thick texture, similar to that of ratatouille, about 15 minutes. A few minutes before finishing, add the freshly squeezed orange juice and taste for salt. Simmer for a minute longer to combine the flavors, then serve alongside Maddalena's Grilled Tuna.

Blood Orange *Gelato*
Makes 1 quart

This incredible *gelato* was created in response to two of my favorite Sicilian foods: creamy *gelato* and the sweet-and-sour blood orange. It has been known to make grown men cry. Do not worry if you can't find blood oranges; the *gelato* is also wonderful made with regular oranges or tangerines.

1 cup sugar
⅛ teaspoon fine sea salt
1 tablespoon very finely shaved or minced lemon zest
2 cups freshly squeezed orange juice (preferably all
*   or at least part blood orange juice)*
3 tablespoons lemon juice (about 1 small lemon)
2½ teaspoons grappa or vodka
⅔ cup heavy cream

Make sure that your ice cream canister is pre-frozen.

Mix together the sugar, salt, and lemon zest (if you have a food processor, use it to thoroughly process the mixture). Add the orange and lemon juice, and stir well to dissolve (again, you could also do this in a food processor). Strain the liquid through a fine-mesh strainer, and then stir in the grappa.

Place the mixture in the freezer to chill for 45 to 60 minutes, stirring occasionally. You want the mixture to become very cold, but you do not want it to freeze.

Whip the cream to soft peaks, and then whisk in the orange mixture. Churn in your ice cream maker until the sherbet develops the texture of soft-serve ice cream. Scoop the sorbet into a different freezable container (for example, a glass loaf pan works well here). Cover with plastic wrap pressed right up against the sorbet, and freeze until hardened, about 3 hours.

Maria

Ricotta non è formaggio. Ricotta è ricotta.

Ricotta is not cheese. Ricotta is ricotta.

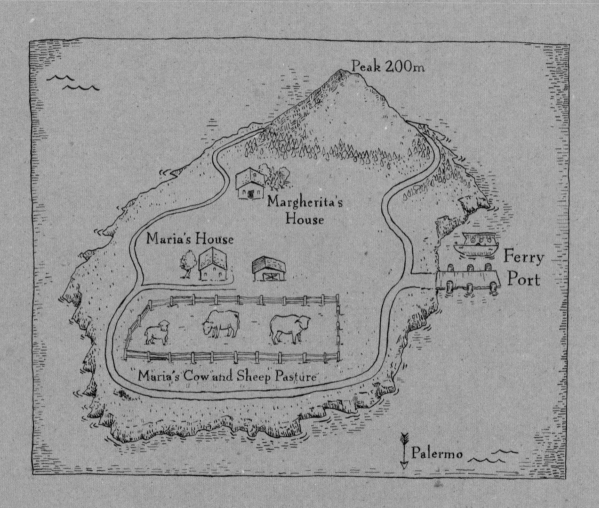

Peak 200m

Margherita's House

Maria's House

Maria's Cow and Sheep Pasture

Ferry Port

Palermo

Ustica, Sicilia

S icily was starting to feel unbearably uncomfortable to me. I was living in Gioiosa Marea, renting a "studio" (converted garage) that a Northern Italian friend had referred me to. It was a pretty grim place: next to the train tracks, inaccessible to much of the island, and lacking in any natural light. Each night, after a long day of driving to visit a new woman or town, I would press the electric button, and the garage door would lurch down at me. The trip to cook with Maddalena had proven fruitful, but I was growing tired of searching for meaningful connections with women on an island so self-protective and guarded.

Then one afternoon I found myself sitting on the fortress above Cefalu, looking through my pink notebook, which I had used to scribble every name and number I'd gathered along my trip. The name Marguerita Longo popped out at me—the pretty young woman all the Bradese boys lusted over at the Slow Food *Congresso* in Naples, almost a year prior. I remembered us having a good conversation, and my liking her and the tiny lentils she grew on the Sicilian island of Ustica. We had decided a visit was in order when I was in Sicily. I decided to call her; it was worth a try.

Marguerita remembered me right away and suggested that I come to stay for a week in her family's agritourism by the ocean. I had nothing else in the calendar for the days ahead. My train would leave Gioiosa Marea for Palermo at five thirty the next morning, and from there I would catch the ferry to Ustica.

Ustica is a small, volcanic island that can only be reached by a blustery hour-long ferry ride from Palermo. Marguerita Longo collected me from the boat terminal and gave me a little driving tour. (A very little tour it was—Ustica mimics its tiny lentils in size. The whole island can be traversed by foot in just over an hour.) The highlight was the ride up to the volcanic peak of the island, with the warm November winds blowing through the broken car windows. We were perched on top of the ocean—Ustica is merely a ledge of land in the middle of water.

Marguerita's mother made us a dinner of lentils, broken pasta, and the last of the summer's tomatoes. She talked about preserving tuna from the annual massacre, of the family's lentils and melons, and of the famed local *ricotta*. Marguerita and her mother asked some questions about my research and decided that an introduction was in order. So, after dinner, Marguerita and I took a walk along the ocean road in the dark; we were going to meet Ustica's cheesemaker, Maria.

The Italian relationship to television never ceased to surprise me. For such a sociable culture, it was odd that in the evenings most Italians could be found gathered silently around the family TV. It was just this way in Maria's house. Marguerita and I walked through the front door of the humble plaster abode, right into the dark kitchen where the cheese was made during the day. There were five or six Usticesi of varying ages in there, all in their house slippers, and all mesmerized by the talking box.

As we entered, Marguerita and I were barely acknowledged. In fact, no one even said *salve* or *buona sera*. Nothing, *niente*. We simply slipped into the circle, standing at first, and then finding seats. We sat quietly for about an hour, and then Marguerita asked if Maria was making cheese the next morning: "Yes, of course!" "Can Jessica come watch?" And so, without a proper introduction, a date was made for six o'clock the following morning. The Usticesi are early risers.

The main thing that stands out from that first day with Maria was just how awkward I felt. Awkwardness had happened from time to time during the previous year, but it came into sharp focus that November morning. I got the feeling that I was too friendly, appreciative, or in awe of her. She seemed perplexed as to why I was watching her, and puzzled by my enthusiasm for her way of life. Or perhaps she was just ignoring me.

When I asked questions, Maria just kept on going. At best I got a gruff grunt of acknowledgment. So I simply watched quietly as she warmed that morning's fresh milk. She added liquid

"We were perched on top of the ocean— Ustica is merely a ledge of land in the middle of water."

An abandoned building along the shores of Ustica.

"Gruff little Maria had been making the same cheese, and the same *ricotta*, for years."

rennet, let the mixture sit for a while, and then gently broke it apart with her hand and scooped up the curds into plastic molds.

When Marguerita and I spoke about Maria over our dinner that night, I learned more about her in ten minutes than I had from Maria herself in three hours. Gruff little Maria had been making the same cheese, and the same *ricotta*, for years. It had become so habitual that she hardly noticed it as skilled, or labor-intensive, or out of the ordinary. It was just what she did, over and over again, week after week, year after year. And there was no one for her to compare herself with. She was, after all, the only cheesemaker on Ustica.

The next morning I made the chilly dawn walk back to Maria's house. The first thing I did wrong that day was simply to ask Maria if she was making the *"ricotta* cheese." The inquiry was met with a scornful and abrupt, *"Ricotta* is not cheese. *Ricotta* is *ricotta."* What on earth is *ricotta* then? I thought. And then I got it. I remembered her setting aside the liquid that had been left over after the curds were strained for yesterday's cheese. Maria had taken the leftover watery whey and let it sit at room temperature for a day and night. As we carried a large sloshing bucket of it to the alcove off the side of the house, I noticed that it had lightly fermented, and was slightly acidic to the nose.

Maria made a strong, wood-burning fire in her hearth, and poured the whey into a large cauldron. Slowly the whey was brought up to a slight simmer. As if by magic, small fluffy white curds began to rise up to the surface of the cauldron. They gathered there, waiting to be scooped out by Maria and her large slotted spoon. Spoonful after spoonful, she strained and tipped them into white conical colanders.

"É acido. É caldo." Somehow in her sparse communication, Maria managed to convey that *ricotta* "happened" from heat and acidity. Later I discovered that the protein albumin, which is abundant in whey, responds to heat and acidity by binding together to form curds. Hence *ricotta*, literally meaning "recooked," is a second cooking of milk. The first cooking, with the addition of rennet (a curdling agent typically obtained from the stomach of a nursing sheep or pig), forms solid "cheese" curds from the milk's casein proteins, leaving behind the watery whey. The

Maria making cheese early one the morning.

second cooking forms curds from the whey's albumin. Two types of protein make for two types of creamy solids, one being cheese and the other being *ricotta*.

It was a short morning, and an hour later I was already walking back down the ocean road with a dripping basket of fluffy *ricotta*. Maria had directed me to eat it her favorite way, on toasted bread with a thick sprinkling of sugar. The *ricotta* was exquisite: creamy, warm, sweet, and ever so slightly sour. Eating it cozied back up in bed, on crunchy bread with crunchy sugar, made it easy to imagine staying on Ustica for a very long time.

I continued to spend time with Maria in the mornings, and then Marguerita and I would make a meal together using the cheese or ricotta later in the day. One lunch we shaved *ricotta salata* over roasted spiky green cauliflower; another time we made a wobbly lemon pudding cake with the soft fresh *ricotta* curds. This was how it went: cheesemaking, cheese cooking, and then cheese talk.

Cheesemaking is a kind of alchemy. This was deeply impressed upon me from watching Maria. From one type of milk, with the addition of one type of rennet, you can make literally hundreds of varieties of cheese. It all depends on how long you leave the rennet in, how you cut the cheese, and the method of aging. With the same two ingredients, anything is possible. Raw milk cheeses, like Maria's, were of particular interest to me. Her cheeses tasted of the local grasses and ocean air, and carried with them all sorts of beneficial enzymes that made their digestion easier.

To my surprise, Marguerita told me that Maria's cheese was illegal; she did not have a license for its production or sale. She had her cows and sheep, and the men in the family would milk them and take them around the fields on the island for pasture. On Tuesdays and Thursdays Maria would make fresh cheeses; some of this was sold soft and young, while other kinds were aged. The *ricotta* was prepared on Wednesdays and Fridays. Everyone bought it. And everyone kept quiet about it.

My last morning on Ustica was spent walking the perimeter of the island. I passed by abandoned stone houses on the cliffs above the ocean, the marine nature preserve, craggy black volcanic rock, and Maria's cows out at pasture. It had been a sharp week, filled with the stink of milk animals, the winter ocean wind, and a feisty little cheesemaker.

Views from my daily walk around the perimeter of Ustica.

Maria : Ustica, Sicilia

Homemade *Ricotta*

Cauliflower and *Ricotta al Forno*

Roasted Green Cauliflower with Saffron, Currants, and *Ricotta Salata*

Two Breakfast Toasts

Fluffed *Ricotta* and Crunchy Sugar

Ricotta al Caffe
(*Ricotta* with Coffee and Honey)

Homemade *Ricotta*

Makes 1–1½ cups ricotta

This is not a true ricotta, true *ricotta* being made from whey, the watery liquid left over after the casein milk solids have been curdled and strained to make cheese. This "ricotta" is a quick and easy cheese made from curdled cream. Its creamy, slightly sour taste serves as a good homemade substitute for traditional *ricotta*.

3¼ cups whole milk (sheep's, goat's, or cow's)
½ cup whipping cream
½ teaspoon salt
2 tablespoons plus 2 teaspoons freshly squeezed, strained lemon juice
1 teaspoon white wine vinegar

Warm the milk, cream, and salt together over medium heat, stirring consistently, until the mixture approaches a simmer. Just before it reaches an active simmer, when the milk starts to foam and undulate, remove it from the heat. Immediately add the lemon juice and vinegar, barely stirring. Let the mixture settle for half an hour. Line a fine mesh colander with two layers of cheesecloth, and place the colander over a bowl; pour in the milk and curds. Allow the "ricotta" to drain for half an hour in the cheesecloth, discarding the liquid that drips from it. Place in the fridge to drip further, until it has reached the consistency you desire—typically ½ to 2 hours more.

Cauliflower and *Ricotta al Forno*

Serves 4–6

This is a creamy, caramelized gratin inspired by Maria's *ricotta* and the abundance of different varieties of cauliflower growing on Ustica. I prefer to use the standard, white cauliflower, to keep this dish a cream color. The comforting gratin would pair beautifully with Mary's roasted rabbit, or Carluccia's braised goat.

½–¾ cup ricotta cheese
⅓ cup heavy cream
1 tablespoon unsalted butter, melted and cooled
¾–1 teaspoon salt
Cracked white or black pepper, a generous pinch
Nutmeg, a few gratings or a pinch
1 cauliflower (about 1½–2 pounds), cut into small florets
⅓ cup grated pecorino or other hard cheese

Preheat the broiler in your oven. Butter a gratin or casserole dish.

In a large bowl, mix together the *ricotta*, cream, butter, salt, pepper, and nutmeg until thoroughly combined.

Boil the cauliflower in salted water until soft and tender, 7 to 10 minutes. Drain and lightly mash it with a fork if you desire, or leave it in small florets. Add the cauliflower to the *ricotta* mixture, stirring well to combine.

Transfer the mixture to the buttered gratin dish. Sprinkle the top of the cauliflower with the grated pecorino. Broil for 5 to 8 minutes, until golden brown.

Roasted Green Cauliflower with Saffron, Currants, and *Ricotta Salata*

Serves 4 as an appetizer or side dish

Ustica was the first place that I saw the spiky green cauliflower commonly known as Romanesco. Marguerita and her mother roasted it for me for lunch one day, shaving slices of Maria's *ricotta salata* (a pressed and salted *ricotta*) over the top. I like to add saffron to this dish, and also currants; adding the currants midway through cooking lends the dish an unexpected, welcome crispiness.

2 generous pinches of saffron threads, about ¼ teaspoon
5 tablespoons olive oil
3 pounds Romanesco or regular cauliflower
½ teaspoon salt
Pinch of crumbled peperoncino
¼ cup currants
¼ cup almonds, coarsely chopped
½ lemon
2 ounces ricotta salata, shaved

Preheat the oven to 400 degrees F. Oil a baking dish large enough to roast the cauliflower in a single layer.

Toast the saffron in a skillet over medium-low heat just until it becomes crumbly and aromatic. Crush in a mortar and mix with the olive oil.

Trim the cauliflower of its stem and any leaves, then cut it lengthwise into ¼-inch-thick slices. Toss the cauliflower with the saffron oil, salt, and peperoncino and lay it in a single layer in the roasting pan. Roast for 15 to 20 minutes or until the cauliflower is cooked through and begins to brown at its edges. Remove the pan from the oven and add the currants and almonds. Bake for 5 to 10 more minutes, or until the cauliflower is nicely caramelized and the almonds are toasted.

Serve either hot or at room temperature. Add a squeeze of lemon and salt to taste. Garnish with generous shavings of *ricotta salata*.

Two Breakfast Toasts

These two toasts were inspired by Maria's preferred early-morning breakfast: thick, fire-grilled toast with warm *ricotta* and sugar. The plain *ricotta* is a simple place to start; the coffee-honey *ricotta* is more exotic, tasting almost like a nutty milk chocolate spread. Both *ricottas* are well suited to toast made with a plain, walnut, or fruit-and-nut bread. They are also delicious used as a filling for *cannoli*, or as a spread for plain tea biscuits.

Fluffed *Ricotta* and Crunchy Sugar
Serves 2

> *½ cup ricotta*
> *2 slices artisan bread, sliced ½ inch thick*
> *½ teaspoon crunchy sugar: turbinado or cane crystals*

Lightly fluff the ricotta by scrambling it with a fork. Toast the bread until browned to your preference. Onto each piece of toast, spoon ¼ cup of ricotta and sprinkle with ¼ teaspoon of sugar.

Ricotta al Caffe (*Ricotta* with Coffee and Honey)
Serves 2

> *½ cup ricotta*
> *1½ teaspoons caster sugar*
> *1 teaspoon honey*
> *¾ teaspoon finely ground coffee*
> *(I use Turkish coffee)*
> *2 slices artisan bread, sliced ½ inch thick*

Sieve the ricotta through a fine-mesh strainer. Mix it with the sugar, honey, and coffee. If the mixture seems grainy, sieve again. While you can eat the *ricotta* right away, the flavors come together wonderfully if left to chill for at least a couple of hours. The coffee *ricotta* will keep in the fridge for a few days.

To serve on toast, toast the bread to your preference and spread ¼ cup of the *ricotta* on top. This *ricotta* is also perfect with simple biscuits and coffee or, in a larger quantity, as a filling for *cannoli*.

AFTERWORD

After my trip to Ustica, I decided to return to Calabria to spend my remaining few weeks in Italy with Carluccia and her happy, hungry family. It had been a year of travel and discovery, and the end of my journey was spent close to the earth, amongst Carluccia's fields of vegetables and animals, grounding all that I had learned. When it came time to fly back to the States, Carluccia sent me off with sacks of her freshly milled flour, a paper bag filled with emerald green chard balls, and a small jar of Tropean red onion marmalade.

I left Italy laden with both physical artifacts and intangible gifts of knowledge. Carluccia's beans and flour came with me, as did the gooey knob of Raffaela's starter. Armida's cast iron testo weighed down my bag, along with pages and pages of notes, hundreds of photographic images, and, of course, the yellow polka dot pajamas that Mamma Maria had given me at the start of my trip. Of the greatest value to me, however, was the wisdom, the friendships, the skills in the kitchen, and the recipes that I had gathered that year.

While it would take me years to fully integrate the depths of learning that occurred for me in Italy, I knew that the best way to begin was to simply cook: to cook in the spirit of these different women, and in close relationship with the seasons and the local land. A few months after my return home, I was nominated by Alice Waters of Chez Panisse for a culinary fellowship at the Montalvo Arts Center, a program designed for emerging chefs dedicated to sustainability. The yearlong fellowship turned into a position as Montalvo's Culinary Curator, work with my most influential culinary mentor, Amaryll Schwertner of Boulettes Larder, and a career in food and health in the San Francisco Bay Area.

What had begun for me decades before as an interest in food for physical health had blossomed in Italy to include food for sheer pleasure, joy, and connection to family and friends and the earth. And, while this was important for my development as a chef, Italy's grandmothers profoundly changed much more than my approach to cooking. At a critical moment in my personal development these wise elder women encircled me with their aprons and lifetimes of experience, and shaped my ability to be a good friend, listener, home-maker, and perhaps someday a wife, mother and even grandmother.

Polpette di Bietola e Marmellata di Cipolla Rossa
(Chard-Sesame Balls and Red Onion Jam)
Serves 6–8 for an appetizer

Although Carluccia was not accustomed to cooking in the early afternoon, when I went to say good-bye she pulled these emerald-green chard balls piping hot from her oven. Out came some Tropean red onion jam and a fizzy glass of the family's red wine to accompany them. It was the perfect, verdant last treat with Carluccia, and she sent me off with an extra paper bag filled with them for the long plane ride home.

For the *polpette*:
2 bunches chard, destemmed and washed
⅓ cup ricotta cheese
¼ cup bread crumbs
2 cloves garlic, very finely minced
⅓ cup finely grated Parmesan or hard pecorino
1 large egg
1 teaspoon lemon zest
Salt to taste
Olive oil
¼–½ cup tan-colored sesame seeds

For the *marmellata*:
1 cup very finely diced white or
*   red onions, or shallots*
¼ cup sugar
Small pinch of salt
Cayenne pepper to taste
1 tablespoon red wine vinegar

To prepare the *marmelatta*, place the onions, sugar, salt, and cayenne together in a small pan. Turn the heat to medium-low, and bring to a boil. The onions will give off significant water—let the mixture boil until it becomes jam-like in consistency, 5 to 10 minutes. Remove from heat and stir in the vinegar. Let cool to room temperature before serving with the warm *polpette*.

To prepare the *polpette*, preheat the oven to 400 degrees F. Lightly oil a baking sheet, or line it with parchment paper. Steam the chard leaves for 2 to 3 minutes. Drain the chard and let briefly cool. Vigorously squeeze the chard dry by turning and pressing it against a fine-mesh strainer repeatedly to strain out the liquid. Finely puree the chard in a food processor. Place a cup of the chard in a large mixing bowl and whisk together with the rest of the ingredients, except for the olive oil and sesame seeds. Place some olive oil in one bowl, and sesame seeds in another. Roll the chard mixture into balls (using about 2 tablespoons per ball). Roll the balls first in the oil and then the sesame seeds. Bake for 20 minutes, until puffed and lightly browned on the bottom.

Giovanna

Mamma Maria

Irene

Armida

Daria

Bruna

Mary

Usha

Italy

Carluccia

Maria

Raffaela

Mediterranean Sea

Maddalena

Jessica's Journey

INDEX

ACKNOWLEDGMENTS

Thank you to all of the extraordinary Italian women who invited me into their kitchens and lives, and generously shared their recipes, stories, and wisdom.

My deep gratitude to Brown University for awarding me the Arnold Fellowship to spend the year in Italy; to Carol Cohen for believing in me and my potential; to the Montalvo Arts Center for giving me the time and space to write; and to Slow Food and Carlo Fanti for helping me get this project off the ground in Italy.

Thank you Alice Waters, for encouraging me to find a way to tell these women's stories and for writing a beautiful introduction to the book; Sarah Weiner, for her unending support and generosity; my agent, Amy Hughes, who was a great guide during this process; Amaryll Schwertner for showing me, by example and through practice, how to be the best chef possible; Zach Hewitt, who's magical illustrations brought so much dimension and charm to the book; Gregory Wakabayashi, the book's designer, for his calm, and his artistry; Lena Tabori, my publisher, who embraced this book from day one; Douglas Gayeton for guiding this book to its perfect home; and my editor, Katrina Fried, for creating that home and bringing out the best that I had to offer in my writing and photography.

While all of my family and friends have helped to make this book possible, there are a few people to whom I am particularly grateful: Sunti, Zina, Pea, Sara, Jane, Ethan, Jonathan, Allison, Beanie, Edward, Mindy, and Mom and Dad—you have all been gifts and beacons in my life; I love you and thank you with all my heart.

A special thanks to Jessie Benthien, an incredible chef and friend, who offered a tremendous amount of help in the development and testing of the recipes in this book. Thank you also to all the other recipe testers who gave of their time and kitchens: Alison Artichoke, Sonya Bibilos, Dan Dill, Michelle Fuerst, Natalie Forsythe, Erika Justis, Sharon Lutz, Sara Maamouri, Ashley Mechling, Sunti Metternich, Angela Moncrief, Pam Nears, Kasey Passen, Allison Post, Sarah Rowntree, Taylor Sperry, Jessica Stokes, Lena Tabori, Vanessa Theroux, Nicole Thomas, Sarah Weiner, Ross Woolen, and Lillian Wright.

J.T., Berkeley, CA

Published in 2010 by Welcome Books®
An imprint of Welcome Enterprises, Inc.
6 West 18th Street, New York, NY, 10011
(212) 989-3200; fax (212) 989-3205
www.welcomebooks.com

Publisher: Lena Tabori
President: H. Clark Wakabayashi
Editor: Katrina Fried
Designer: Gregory Wakabayashi
Illustrator: Zach Hewitt

ISBN: 978-1-59962-089-3

Library of Congress Cataloging-in-Publication Data

Theroux, Jessica.
   Cooking with italian grandmothers : recipes and stories from Tuscany to Sicily / by Jessica Theroux ; Introduction by Alice Waters.
      p. cm.
   ISBN 978-1-59962-089-3 (hardcover)
   1. Cookery, Italian. I. Title.
   TX723.T476 2010
   641.5945—dc22

                                    2010021657

First Edition
10 9 8 7 6 5 4 3 2 1

PRINTED IN CHINA

For further information about this book please visit online:
www.welcomebooks.com/cookingwithitaliangrandmothers

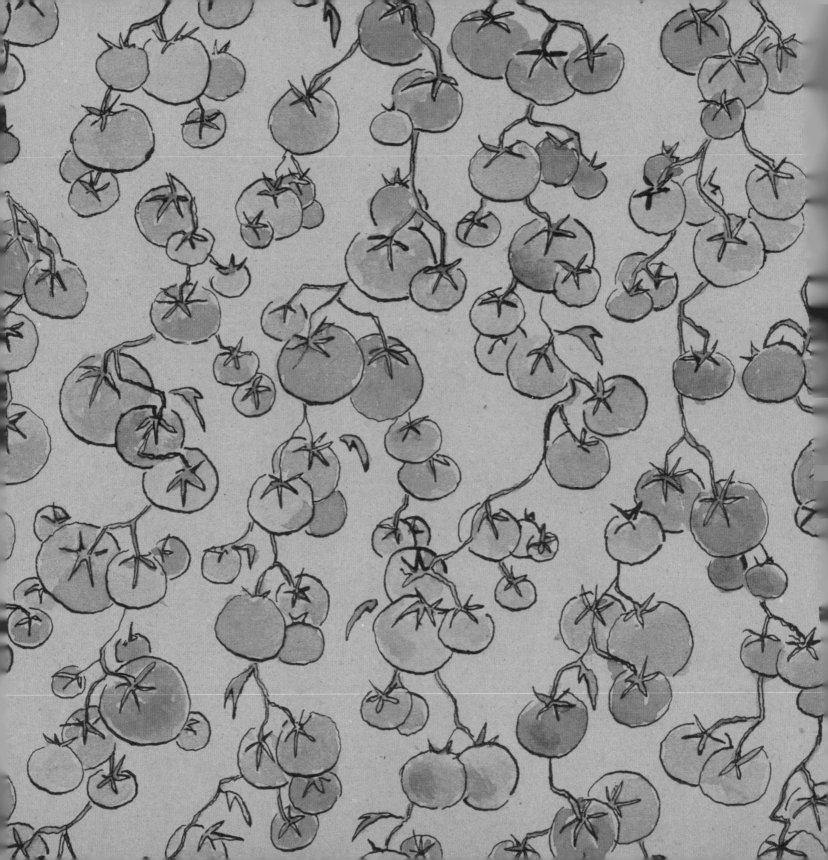